Buon Ricordo

Buon Ricordo

Armando Percuoco
and
David Dale

Photographs by Greg Elms

ALLEN&UNWIN

How to make your home a great restaurant

This edition published in 2011

First published in 2009

Allen & Unwin

83 Alexander Street

Crows Nest NSW 2065

Australia

Phone: (61 2) 8425 0100

Fax: (61 2) 9906 2218

Email: info@allenandunwin.com

Web: www.allenandunwin.com

Cataloguing-in-Publication details are available from the National Library of Australia www.librariesaustralia.nla.gov.au

ISBN 978 1 74237 487 1

Project management by Mary Trewby

Text design by Marylouise Brammer

Photography by Greg Elms

Styling by Virginia Dowzer

Colour reproduction by Splitting Image, Clayton, Victoria

Printed in China by 1010 Printing International Limited

10 9 8 7 6 5 4 3 2 1

contents

Welcome

During 30 years of running restaurants in Australia I've watched a society transform itself. When I started, the only thing Australians knew about Italian food was spaghetti bolognese. Now they order the most adventurous dishes with perfect pronunciation. It's been a joy to serve so many open-minded diners.

But while Australians have become sophisticated restaurant customers, they remain sadly distanced from their food when they're at home. They understand the cuisines of many nations. They know eight different ways to ask for coffee. But at home their confidence seems to vanish. Suddenly cooking becomes a chore and eating a solitary pleasure. We may eat out together but we eat in apart. Families don't share meals and, as a consequence, they don't talk. We've become a fragmented society.

I think we can rebuild community around the table. And I think Italian food is the way to achieve that. It's the most accessible, generous and participatory cooking style in the world. Even an absolute beginner can produce meals that are satisfying and impressive. And cooking creates conversation.

I may be doing myself out of a job, but I want to remove the mystique from restaurant food, to make you feel as comfortable in your kitchen as I feel in the kitchen of Buon Ricordo (which means 'fond memory'). This book shows you how to cook great Italian food in many different ways. I hope that you and the people you cook with will come to understand the ingredients, know when they're at their best and learn how different techniques can bring out different qualities in them.

Chapter 1 introduces my favourite ingredients and a notion that seems radical to some—for everything there is a season, and when it's not that season, you should cook something else. Most of the dishes in Chapter 2—which is about mucking about in the kitchen with friends and family—can be made by your kids, with a little help from their adult slaves. Chapter 3 is a collection of classics that I grew up with and have adapted slightly for modern times. Chapter 4 is all about showing off—spectacular creations that will cause your guests to say you should open your own restaurant. All Italian food is healthy, but Chapter 5 is even better for you than the rest of the book: it's full of good-looking vegetarian dishes and food low in fat and sugar. And Chapter 6 reveals how we eat in Buon Ricordo when the customers can't see us—a bunch of big tasty feasts for chaotic casual gatherings.

Now we're ready to cook—and to eat—together. *Buon appetito e buon ricordo.*

1
basic beginnings

When I was growing up in Naples, my parents followed a division of labour that proved very useful to me in later life. My father did the shopping and my mother did the cooking.

I would go to the markets with Dad and watch him choose the freshest fish, the fruits, vegetables and leaves that were at their seasonal peaks, and the tastiest cuts of meat for our modest budget. Back at home, I'd join my brothers and sisters in helping Mum turn those ingredients into sauces and salads and stews and puddings. Then we'd sit down to a family meal full of big flavours and loud conversation.

It was inevitable that I would end up in the business of feeding people. My great-grandparents and my grandparents had run restaurants and cafés. My father was one of the most respected head waiters in Naples. My family name, Percuoco, literally translates as 'for a cook'.

At the age of 14 I started work as a waiter, and went through a rigorous training in how to keep the customer happy. Then my curiosity took me into the kitchen, where I learned how to turn out interesting meals for large numbers of people in limited time.

In 1972 I travelled to Australia to join my parents and in 1979 we opened a restaurant called Pulcinella in Sydney's Kings Cross. At first I was frustrated that so few of the ingredients we took for granted in Italy were available here. We had to content ourselves with our best approximations of the traditional dishes I'd grown up with. But I was excited that the customers were so open to new ideas and that growers and suppliers were becoming more adventurous with products.

By 1987 I felt I could open a more ambitious restaurant, offering a higher standard of service and a more imaginative approach. I decided to call it Buon Ricordo. I wanted to take *la cucina Italiana* to the next level. This book explains how I did it.

I've learned that cooking, like life, was meant to be easy. By applying the Italian principles of freshness, simplicity and generosity, anyone can create meals that will satisfy family and entertain friends.

In this book I have tried to give precise measurements, but my hope is that you will improvise. Experiment with flavours. If you like more garlic, less chilli, more parsley, less pepper, follow your palate—not my instructions. That's how Italians do it, whether they're at home or in a restaurant kitchen.

It all begins with the ingredients, and here I discuss some of my favourites.

The core elements of my cooking

In some parts of Australia it may be a challenge to source some foodstuffs. A few of the ingredients here may be unfamiliar to your local greengrocer, butcher, deli or fishmonger. So push them. Show them the recipe and ask them to order the ingredient. Bring the storekeepers into your conversation and tell them how it went when you've made the dish.

Olive oil (*olio d'oliva*)

When I first came to Australia the olive oil we used was always imported from Italy. Now we can be proud of our home-grown oil. I use mainly Australian oil in my restaurant—I grow the olives myself on my farm north of Sydney.

I love looking out from my farmhouse to the line of gum trees behind my rows of olive trees. That's when I think of myself as a proud Italian–Australian and a proud Australian–Italian, and I reflect on how much this country has changed in four decades.

Of course, in some recipes I need the particular flavour of an oil from a region of Italy. A cook needs a broad repertoire of ingredients.

The bitterness or sweetness of the oil depends on which olives were used in its making. On my farm the oil is made from corrigiola, leccino and pendolino olives, which make a mellow fruity blend. It's fun to become your own oil maker—shop around, taste a variety of oils to determine what you like best and mix them to make your personal blend. Some people like their oil peppery (Tuscan style) and some like it mellow (as the Ligurians do). Peppery oils are good for salads. For splashing on steamed fish, a mellower oil is better.

There are a lot of myths about olive oil. There's no reason to use 'extra virgin' in cooking—it's expensive and it can make the dish too heavy. A bottle simply labelled 'olive oil', with no claims about virginity or cold pressing, is good enough for frying, provided you like the taste. Save the extra virgin for drizzling on salads and soups, and to splash on pasta as you serve it.

Olive oil is no better if it's deep green in colour—that just means the makers included a few leaves when they were crushing the olives.

Oils from the Southern Hemisphere are bottled between March and May. Although they are best when new, they do stay good for months. Olive oil is like having a lover—best to change it for a fresh one every year and best to keep it secret. If it's kept in the dark, a good oil can last up to 18 months before going rancid.

Some recipes call for deep-frying. You can use olive oil for this (never extra virgin) or a vegetable oil such as canola. I recommend deep-frying in a wok rather than a flat-bottomed pan because you can achieve the necessary depth without using so much oil. Before you start cooking, make sure the oil is hot enough that it sizzles when a drop of water is thrown in.

Bruschetta • I've been putting a tomato topping on toast and giving it to my customers at the start of their meals for the past 20 years—it's my biggest secret. • Put a tomato into boiling water for 2 minutes, peel off the skin, chop into small cubes and marinate it for an hour in extra virgin olive oil, chopped basil and finely chopped garlic. When you're ready to serve, sprinkle on a little salt and spoon the tomato onto a thin slice of toasted Italian bread.

Napoletana sauce • Thump a clove of garlic with the heel of your hand, remove the skin and sauté it in a saucepan with about 3 tablespoons of olive oil over high heat until it turns golden, about 2 minutes. Add 400 g (13 oz) of chopped tomatoes (they can be tinned) and cook, uncovered, over medium heat for 8 minutes. Add 10 chopped basil leaves and simmer for another 2 minutes. Taste and add salt as necessary. Remove the garlic clove. You will end up with about 2 cups of sauce.

Tomatoes (*pomodori*)

Winter or summer, please don't put tomatoes in the fridge. If they are not ripe the cold will stop their ripening, and if they are ripe the cold will cut their flavour. Tomatoes are the opposite of olive oil—they are best kept in the sunlight.

There is one sauce I'll mention often in this book: Napoletana. You can make it in 12 minutes, and any left over can be kept for a couple of days in the fridge. Every household in Naples has oil, garlic, tomatoes and a bunch of fresh basil as part of their basic kitchen supplies, so they can throw together a Napoletana at any time. The sauce can go on pasta or pizza or a piece of fish just as it is, or it can be one of many elements in a more complex dish, such as the *Timballo* on page 143.

Tomatoes are always improved with the addition of a little salt but, whether they are cooked or raw, don't add the salt until just before you're serving them. If it's added too early, the salt makes the tomatoes watery.

Some recipes call for tomatoes that have been peeled and seeded. Put the tomatoes in boiling water for 2 minutes, drain and then peel off the skin. To remove the seeds, cut the tomatoes in half and scoop out the seeds with your finger or a teaspoon.

Remember that tomatoes are highly seasonal and at their best in mid to late summer. You can buy them all year round, but it's rare in winter to find tomatoes good enough to serve as a salad. And if you're making Napoletana sauce in winter, it's better to use the tinned variety (ideally from San Marzano, near Naples).

Tomato salads • Cut ripe tomatoes in quarters and toss them with extra virgin olive oil and finely sliced basil leaves. • Cut ripe tomatoes into discs and toss them with finely sliced red onions, extra virgin olive oil and dried oregano. Just before serving, add salt and freshly ground black pepper.

Onions and garlic (*cipolle e aglio*)

Many of my sauces begin with a *soffritto* of onions or garlic gently fried in olive oil—but rarely both together. Each makes a different contribution to a dish. Some Italians believe onions go best with meat and garlic goes with fish, though there are exceptions to this. The important details are always start with the oil at room temperature, and toss in the finely sliced onions or garlic before you apply the heat. That way they'll warm up gradually and won't become burnt or bitter.

Garlic needs only 2–3 minutes cooking to become golden, before you start adding other ingredients. In some of my recipes I suggest you cook a whole garlic clove in oil but remove it before serving, so that it doesn't overpower the flavour. In others, sliced garlic is an important part of the sauce. The best garlic is locally grown or Italian. Try to avoid the big Russian or Chinese bulbs.

Onions need more cooking than garlic—at least 10 minutes to bring out their sweetness. Stir them often with a wooden spoon to ensure they don't stick to the pan and burn. If you fry them gently in extra virgin olive oil for 90 minutes, you can make a fine onion jam which can be kept in the fridge for adding to dishes later.

And here's a piece of advice I'm going to repeat often in this book—don't add salt until the end of the cooking process. If you add it early, it will pull the water out of the onions and spoil the texture and flavour of the dish.

Herbs (*erbe*)
The main herbs I use are parsley, basil and oregano. The rule with herbs is to add them at the end of the cooking process. If you heat them for too long they can lose their flavour or become bitter. The only exception to this principle is bay leaves, which can (and should) be cooked for hours in a soup or stew.

Parsley is, of course, the fresh European flat-leaf variety (also known as Italian parsley). I chop it finely and sprinkle it on most of my pasta dishes and many main courses, particularly fish. In this book I've used measures such as a 'tablespoon' of finely chopped parsley or a 'handful' of parsley leaves, but these are meant to be very approximate measures. I suggest that you always have a bunch in the fridge and when you're making one of my dishes, chop as many leaves as suit your taste. The only use I can think of for the frizzy English type of parsley is deep-fried, to add crunch to a plate of mixed fried seafood.

Dried basil is horrible. Fresh basil can now be bought all year round but, like tomatoes, it is at its best in mid to late summer. The out-of-season version has much bigger leaves and tastes less interesting—but it's still good enough for sprinkling on tomato-flavoured dishes. With any mixed salad you should toss in a few leaves of basil. It gives lettuce another dimension.

Oregano can be fresh or dried, depending on the dish. Fresh oregano has a milder flavour and is beautiful with fish because it doesn't dominate. But the dried herb is ideal with tomatoes because its sharpness accentuates their flavour. Oregano, whether fresh or dried, should be added to a sauce about 5 minutes before the end of the cooking process.

Fresh mint goes best with ingredients that are fried and then marinated in vinegar. Its sharpness cuts the oiliness.

Rosemary is fantastic with roasted meats, especially with lamb and poultry. Thyme leaves are a wonderful flavour-booster for fish and are better fresh than dried.

Salad (*insalata*)

I like to serve vegetables with meat dishes and salad leaves with fish. My favourite leaves are radicchio and rocket because they have much more character than lettuce.

Radicchio should be red and bitter and eaten in winter. It goes well with fennel, another great winter ingredient. When you're tired of raw radicchio you can grill or bake it.

Dark green rocket (which we Italians call *rucola*) comes in broad leaves and in long thin leaves—I think the thinner rocket has more flavour. To me, rocket is perfect with T-bone steak.

Grilled or baked radicchio
• Grill the radicchio on an oiled hot plate or in a frying pan with a little olive oil for 2 minutes each side, which brings up the sweetness. •
Or wrap a few radicchio leaves in prosciutto and barbecue the bundles for 2 minutes each side, or put the bundles in a frying pan with a little olive oil over high heat for 2 minutes each side, to crisp up the prosciutto wrapping.

Vegetables (*contorni*)

Italians like their pasta to be *al dente* and their vegetables mushy. They are wrong about the second part. If you overcook vegetables you lose their colour, goodness and flavour. So forget the Italians and listen to me. Here are a few thoughts on the best ways to treat the kind of vegetables that will go with the dishes in this book.

Asparagus (*asparagi*) Cut off the ends and lightly peel the skin (with a potato peeler) below the tip. For a barbecued taste, put a little olive oil in a non-stick frying pan and fry the asparagus over high heat for 7 minutes. Serve with only salt and pepper. Or steam the asparagus for 10 minutes with a little water in a covered pot, then sprinkle on freshly grated parmesan cheese and pour a little melted butter over just before serving.

Beans (*fagioli*) Italians embrace beans in a huge variety of colours and textures. In spring we love fresh fava (broad) beans—we peel off the skins and eat them raw or steam them for just a minute or two (splashed with extra virgin olive oil, of course). Dried beans such as cannellini should be soaked overnight in a lot of water, drained and then boiled in more water for about 45 minutes, until they are tender. They are great mixed with chopped tomatoes and served with salami or a salty cheese and extra virgin olive oil.

With green beans, boil them for no more than 5 minutes and then put them straight into cold water to stop the cooking process. Toss them in lemon juice and olive oil—with a little chopped garlic, if you like—just before you serve them.

Broccoli Steam the florets of broccoli for 5 minutes; sauté some finely chopped garlic in olive oil for about 1 minute, then add the steamed broccoli, toss and serve immediately. To boost the flavour even more, you can mash an anchovy into the oil before you start cooking the garlic.

Cabbage (*verzi*) If you suffer from the prejudice that cabbage is boring, you probably haven't cooked it for long enough to release the sugars—at least 10 minutes. You could try spicing it up with chilli and white wine to make a dish we call *verzi con peperoncino*.

Verzi con peperoncino • Fry a whole garlic clove and a small, finely chopped red chilli in a frying pan with olive oil for 2 minutes. Toss in a whole chopped cabbage, stir with a wooden spoon and cook for a further 4 minutes. Then pour in 1 glass of white wine and ½ glass of water, cover and cook over low heat for 20 minutes. Remove the garlic before you serve the cabbage in a big bowl with a sprinkle of parsley and a little salt.

If you still think it's boring, try the sharper form we call cavolo nero—which literally means 'black cabbage'. It's often translated in this country as 'Tuscan kale', but I don't see why the Tuscans should get all the credit.

Capsicums (*peperoni*) To improve the flavour of the capsicums you have to burn their skins until they are black. You can do this on a barbecue or under a griller, but I suggest you turn a gas flame on your stove up to maximum and put the whole capsicum onto it. Using tongs, keep turning the capsicum around for at least 3 minutes until the skin is burnt on all sides. Then put the capsicum on a board and, once it is cool enough to handle, cut off the top, remove all the seeds

and pull the blackened skin off with your fingers. Slice the flesh into strips and splash on a little extra virgin olive oil. Don't put the scorched capsicum in water at any point or you will lose some of the sweet flavour that comes from the burning.

Chillies (*peperoncini*) The northern Italians don't use much chilli, but we like it in the south because it seems to match our climate.

I suggest you use small red chillies rather than big ones, and only include the seeds if you insist on a fiery taste (which is likely to knock out everything else). The important thing is to put the finely sliced chilli in the pan at the beginning, along with the garlic, so it's thoroughly infused in the sauce.

Eggplants (*melanzane*) The longer you cook eggplants, the better they taste. There are different varieties for different purposes. In this book I concentrate on the large ones, which can be cut into discs and layered with cheese and Napoletana sauce (see recipe, page 20). Older cookbooks used to suggest you reduced the bitterness of the eggplants by cutting them into slices, sprinkling them with salt and draining off their juices. But, thanks to advances in breeding, that's no longer necessary. If you cut an eggplant in half and find lots of black seeds, throw it away because it's too old.

Endives (*scarole*) Endives are long curly green leaves attached to a bulb (see the photograph opposite)—not to be confused with witlof or Belgium endive. They are good in salads and give great texture and flavour chopped up in soups. But endives are tough if undercooked, so boil them for at least half an hour if you want to serve them on pizza or as an antipasto (fry the boiled endives with garlic and olive oil for 2 minutes, then stir in olives, pine nuts, raisins and anchovies).

Peas (*piselli*) Peas go wonderfully as a side dish with meat, pasta and rice. Cooked with onions and bacon, they can also be served as part of an antipasto spread. But remember, they are seasonal and at their best in spring and early summer. Outside the season, the peas you find at the greengrocer can be pale, hard and nasty, and you'd be better off using frozen peas. Just cook the frozen peas for about half the time you'd cook the fresh ones (4 minutes after they've come to the boil, rather than 8). Please don't use dried or tinned peas.

Potatoes (*patate*) As an accompaniment to a roast or grill, use new potatoes cut into pieces about the size of a golf ball. First boil them for 5 minutes, then put them in a baking dish with cloves of peeled garlic and a couple of twigs of rosemary and a couple of splashes of olive oil. Roast them in a 200°C (400°F/gas 6) oven for 15 minutes.

Peas as antipasto • Cook shelled peas in boiling water for 8 minutes. Meanwhile, fry a finely chopped onion and a little bacon in olive oil for about 10 minutes. Drain the peas and add them to the onion, stir and fry for another 4 minutes. At the last minute, throw in some chopped fresh mint (or parsley if you're not a mint lover).

And if you're making mashed potatoes, mix them with freshly grated parmesan cheese and extra virgin olive oil instead of the butter and milk the French would use. Don't be tempted to try to puree potatoes in a blender—that gives a terrible texture. Put your shoulder into the job with a heavy fork or masher, or use a potato ricer.

Zucchini Dice some zucchini, steam for 4 minutes, then marinate for at least an hour in extra virgin olive oil, finely chopped garlic and roughly chopped fresh mint leaves. That's a fine side dish. Or fry strips in very hot olive oil and serve them crunchy.

As for zucchini flowers, I prefer the male ones because they have a better flavour. The male grows directly on the vine; the female is on the end of the zucchini. Some people like to use yellow pumpkin flowers instead of the light green and yellow zucchini flowers, but I find they are often bitter. It's strange to think that when I first arrived in Australia, the growers used to throw the zucchini flowers away. Nowadays every chef stuffs them with cheeses and nuts and other elements that, to me, distract from their delicate flavour. I prefer them without filling, quickly fried in a little light batter.

Figs (*fichi*)

I'm told that in the 1950s every Australian backyard had a fig tree but they were regarded more as a nuisance than a delicacy to be looked forward to in late summer. Europeans use them in many different ways—fresh as an entrée or cooked as a side vegetable or as a dessert. I prefer black mandolin-shaped figs—they stay firmer when cooked.

Pasta

Most Italians use dried pasta most of the time, and in this book I only suggest you make your own pasta for one recipe—a ravioli. Otherwise, my sauces go perfectly well with bought pasta.

Most Australian-made commercial pasta is not up to the standard of the Italian version. You should spend a couple of dollars extra and buy Italian pasta made with durum wheat. Check on the packet to see if the pasta has been pressed through bronze moulds: it should say *al bronzo*. The bronze moulds give a texture to the surface which holds the sauce better than smooth pasta.

Shape matters. Long noodle-type pasta, such as spaghetti and linguine, go best with seafood. Wider pasta—fettucine, pappardelle and tagliatelle, for example—or tube pasta, like penne and rigatoni, go better with meat sauces or vegetable sauces.

I usually like to cook the sauce and boil the pasta at the same time, and to slightly undercook the pasta—until it's almost *al dente*, or 'firm to the bite'. I drain it and throw it into the pan with the sauce for a minute or so, stirring so it absorbs some of the liquid in the pan.

I also like to make what Italians call pasta *in brodo* or *minestra*—a kind of soup that is thickened by adding the tiny pieces of pasta we call *tubetti* or the broken bits of spaghetti or pappardelle.

Fig salad • Cut figs in half, sprinkle on brown sugar and place in a baking dish. Bake them in a 180°C (350°F/ gas 4) oven for 5 minutes. Splash on a bit of olive oil and good aged balsamic vinegar and serve them with mesclun leaves or with endive.

Which brings me to Australia's national dish—spag bol. It does not exist in Italy. In Bologna, where supposedly it was invented, they would never dream of serving their slow-cooked meat sauce (called *ragú*) with spaghetti. They know it needs to be delivered to the palate via a ribbon pasta such as fettucine or tagliatelle.

Do the experiment yourself: make a bolognese sauce and then try some on spaghetti and some on fettucine. You'll find that the ribbon pasta version is more satisfying. Then you'll be ready to join me in my campaign to change Australia's national dish from spag bol to fettucine *al ragú*.

Polenta

This is a powder made of milled corn, which is turned into a kind of porridge with water and/or stock. It can be served soft or hard, boiled, fried, baked or grilled. The soft version is great served with stewed meat. Some 'instant' varieties are available but I find they lack the texture of the traditional kind, which needs to be stirred constantly.

To cook the polenta, pour it in a steady stream into a pot of boiling water (or a mixture of half water, half chicken stock) and then keep stirring for 45 minutes. The only additives you need at the beginning are salt and bay leaves, but towards the end you can grate in some parmesan or provola cheese or even throw in a few pieces of salami or cooked sausage.

If you want to turn the polenta into crunchy wedges, put a little olive oil on a baking tray, pour in the polenta and bake in a preheated 180°C (350°F/gas 4) oven for 40 minutes. That turns it into a cake, which you can slice. To make it really crisp, dip the slices into beaten egg whites and deep-fry them in olive oil until they turn golden, about 5 minutes, then season with salt and pepper. Eat them as snacks with beer or wine, or use them as a base for lively toppings, such as salty anchovies, onion jam, ricotta mixed with a little Spanish onion and olive oil, or the tomato topping I put on my bruschetta (see page 20).

Stock (*sugo di carne*)

In Italy, we boil bones to make broth (into which we throw vegetables and small bits of pasta). We also make stock to enrich sauces. There are reasonably good liquid stocks available now, but making your own and keeping a supply in the freezer is more satisfying. I make a rich

Venison jus • Roughly chop 1 onion, 1 carrot, 2 sticks of celery and 4 bay leaves. Put them in a large saucepan with 3 tablespoons of olive oil and fry for 5 minutes over high heat. Throw in 1 kg (2 lb) of venison bones (or beef bones) and a handful of juniper berries and fry for a further 5 minutes, stirring often. Fill the saucepan with water, bring to the boil, lower the heat and simmer uncovered for 5 hours. Strain the stock, discarding the bones and vegetables. Reduce for another hour to thicken, skimming any scum off the top. Add salt to your taste. Cool, then pour into a bowl, cover and store in the freezer until you're ready to use it.

venison stock that can be used as a sauce on beef or lamb dishes—
you need to ask the butcher to order venison bones. If he swears he
can't find them, ask for beef bones, preferably joints and legs. The
method opposite is for venison *jus* (used on page 157).

Cheese (*formaggio*)

Parmesan is as ubiquitous in this book as it is in Italy. It even boosts
the flavour of prawns in one of my creations. But I have to be strict
about it. Only buy Italian parmesan. Australians can do many things,
but they can't make the cheeses Italians know as *parmigiano reggiano*

and *grana padana*. Parmesan doesn't always have to be grated. It is wonderful served in chunks with hard red pears.

Next in my favourite cheeses list comes *fior di latte*—a name you may be unfamiliar with until I tell you it's often called mozzarella. In Italy mozzarella is made with buffalo milk and the version made with cow's milk is called *fior di latte* (literally, 'flower of milk'). You would never waste buffalo mozzarella on pizza because it melts away, whereas *fior di latte* softens but stays together. Good *fior di latte* may not be as creamy as mozzarella *di bufala*, but it should be white, not yellow. Avoid the type that looks and tastes like a big rubber ball.

And third comes provola, which has a meaty taste and stands up well to heat, especially the smoked version. Provola can be bought as a ball, which you can slice in thick slabs and sear on a barbecue, then serve with Napoletana sauce.

A couple of my recipes call for gorgonzola. I prefer *dolcelatte,* the mild version, rather than the strong blue version. I also like the soft sweet cheese called taleggio. If you can't find it, substitute fontina.

Equipment

The most important tools in the kitchen are your hands. After that, to make the most of this book you'll need:

- several sizes of sharp knives: large for chopping, thin and long for filleting, small for peeling and finely slicing, plus a bread knife
- heavy-based saucepan (not aluminium) large enough to hold at least 2 litres (72 fl oz) of liquid
- frying pans, both non-stick and cast iron, able to be used in an oven (make sure they're ovenproof). If you have a new cast-iron pan you should cure it: coat with a little olive oil and put in a very hot oven for 30 minutes. Use gloves when taking it out of the oven, then wash it and coat with oil. And whenever you wash the pan, rub it with oil again to prevent rust
- strainer for pasta and some sheets of fine muslin for straining the grit out of stocks before you make sauces
- potato ricer—to mash potatoes
- fish slice
- wooden spoons
- cheese grater

- metal pan about 40 cm (16 inches) across for pizza
- blender
- tongs and ladles
- meat mallet for flattening veal and beef
- wok (or deep-sided frying pan) for deep-frying—I recommend a wok because it requires less oil
- stainless steel or copper saucepans, about 23 cm (9 inches) and 20 cm (8 inches) in diameter
- oval stainless steel or copper dish about 30 cm (12 inches) long
- range of metal moulds, ramekins, soufflé dishes, springform cake tins and tart tins in various sizes
- range of serving platters of different sizes
- shears for cutting chicken and quail
- big board for rolling out dough (marble if possible).

2

family fun

Picture a family sitting round the dining table at 7 pm on a typical week night eating a meal that has been cooked mostly by the kids, with a bit of help from Mum, Dad and Nan. The children are talking excitedly about what happened at school, what they're looking forward to on TV later, and the newest discoveries they've made about what foods go with what other ingredients to make a brilliant meal. The adults are praising the young ones for their kitchen skills.

Here's another picture. Mum and Dad are in front of the TV with cartons of takeaway Thai on their laps. In another room, the kids are sitting in front of computer terminals gnawing at slices of pizza from a greasy cardboard box on the desk next to them. Grandma's in the kitchen looking in the fridge to see if there's anything worth eating. There isn't.

How do we turn the first image into reality for the majority of households? By convincing children that cooking can be as much of a pleasure as eating.

We start with pizza, and I'll soon convince you that your kids will have no trouble making a twenty-first century adaptation of the dish invented near Naples more than two thousand years ago. Their version will be ten times tastier than any cardboard creation that might be delivered to your door.

These are recipes for family occasions—summer lunches, winter dinners, parties, brunches and barbecues. They are both sophisticated and simple. Some of them will involve a lot of mess in the kitchen. That's part of the process of transforming the takeaway lovers into good and happy cooks.

If this very Italian notion of family and friends cooking and eating and talking together can spread through the English-speaking world, I like to hope there will be two results: first, it might alleviate the problem of obesity and ill-health among children, because kids will learn to understand what they're eating and appreciate that good things can taste good; and secondly, it might reduce the problems of isolation and alienation in modern society.

A happy nation is built upon happy relationships—and happy relationships are built in the kitchen and around the dining table. This chapter is the beginning of my crusade. Please join me.

1. **Calzone** Folded pizza

2. **Pizza di famiglia** The big pizza

3. **Fiori fritti** Fried zucchini flowers

4. **Insalata di mozzarella estiva** *Fior di latte* cheese with capsicum

5. **Insalata di arance sanguinelle** Blood orange salad

6. **Uova con provola alla pizzaiola** Poached eggs with provola and spicy sauce

7. **Crocchette** Potato croquettes

8. **Pomodoro con pere al balsamico** Tomato and pear salad with prosciutto rolls

9. **Crema di broccoli** Broccoli soup

10. **Brodo di pollo** Chicken broth with fennel

11. **Quattro piccole paste** Four little pastas

12. **San Pietro con crema di piselli** John Dory with pea puree

13. **Grigliata mista di mare** Seafood barbecue

14. **Bistecca alla fiorentina all'Armando** T-bone steak, my way

15. **Grigliata mista di carne** Mixed grill

16. **Galletto alla diavola** Peppered spatchcock

17. **Ragú** The Sunday feast

18. **Scaloppine alla caprese** Veal with eggplant

19. **Costoletta alla Teano** Schnitzel with eggplant *parmigiana*

20. **Granita di limo** Lime granita

21. **Pesche in vino rosso** Yellow peaches in red wine

22. **Semifreddo** Not quite ice-cream

23. **Zabaglione** Egg nog

24. **Mascarpone** Cream cheese sundae

25. **Torta mascarpone** Cherry cake

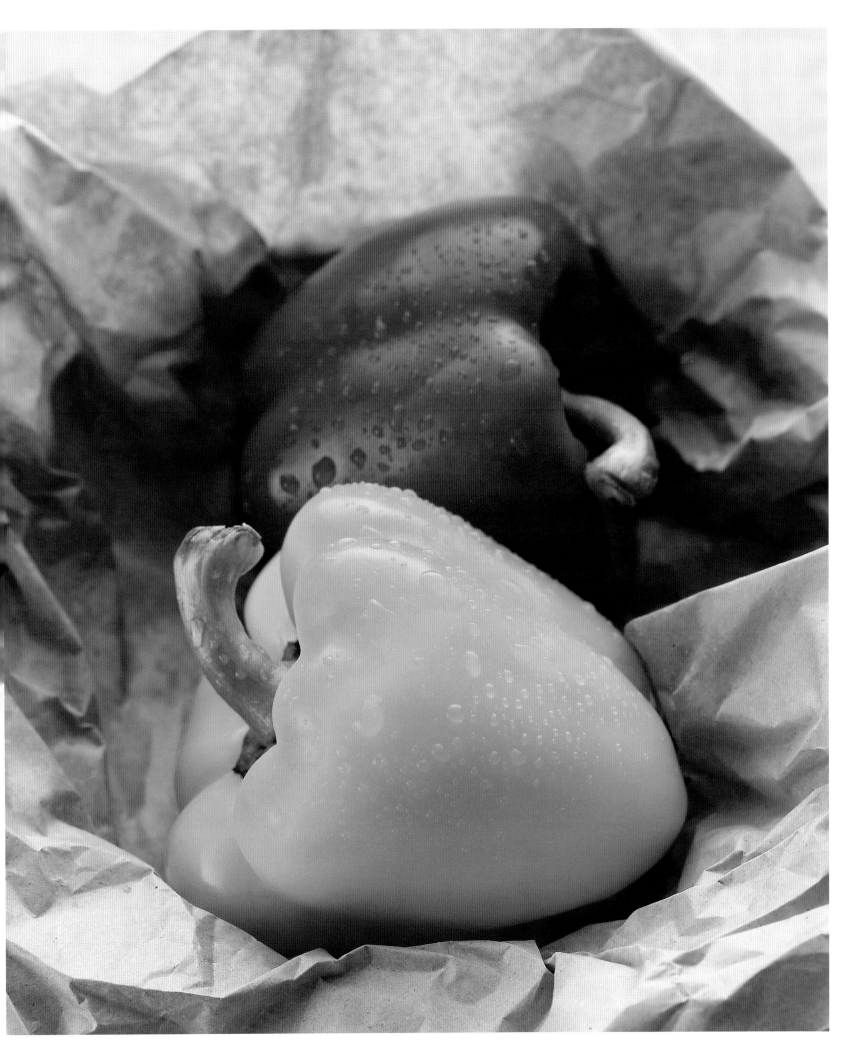

Let's start with individual pizza parcels, known as calzone. If you can't find fresh yeast at your supermarket, you can buy it at health food stores and bakeries. A warning: do not add salt because it will stop the action of the yeast. The salt is added only after the dough rises.

For the filling I've suggested ricotta, chopped salami and strong provolone cheese, but you can experiment. Chopped ham or cooked bacon can replace the salami. Or you can do a vegetarian version using chopped spinach instead of salami. It's up to you.

1. Calzone
Folded pizza

500 g (1 lb) flour
20 g (¾ oz) fresh yeast
olive oil for frying
150 g (5 oz) freshly grated
    parmesan cheese
basil leaves for serving

FOR THE SAUCE
5 tbsp olive oil
2 cloves garlic, finely chopped
400 g (13 oz) tomatoes, chopped
10 basil leaves, chopped

FOR THE FILLING
300 g (10 oz) ricotta cheese
150 g (5 oz) salami, finely diced
150 g (5 oz) provola cheese, diced
4 tbsp freshly grated parmesan
    cheese
salt and freshly ground black
    pepper

Place the flour in a mound on a benchtop and make a well in the centre. Crumble the yeast into the centre and pour over ½ cup of warm water to dissolve the yeast. With your hands, mix the flour and yeast together and knead. Add more warm water if necessary to create a wet dough. Knead until the dough feels elastic. Form it into a ball and put it aside to rest in a warm place for at least 1 hour.

While the dough is resting, make the sauce. Put the olive oil and garlic in a saucepan over medium heat and let the garlic sizzle until golden, about 2 minutes. Add the chopped tomatoes and cook for 8 minutes. At the last minute, stir in the basil, leaving a few leaves for the garnish. Set aside.

Sprinkle flour on the benchtop, knead the dough again and, with a rolling pin, flatten it out to a thickness of about 1 cm (½ inch). Cut out circles of dough about 10 cm (4 inches) wide by cutting round a side plate to get the shape, making as many as you can. Place the dough on a baking tray.

For the filling, mix the ricotta, salami, provola and parmesan. Add salt and pepper to taste. Place 2 tablespoons of the filling on one half of each circle of dough, then fold the other half across to make a half-moon shape. Press all around the edges with a finger or fork.

Heat 6 cm (2½ inches) of olive oil in a wok or deep frying pan until it sizzles when a little piece of dough is thrown in. Fry the calzone until golden, about 5 minutes. Remove and drain on paper towels.

When all the calzone are cooked, place them on a serving dish, pour over a generous spoonful of the sauce, and sprinkle over the freshly grated parmesan cheese and a little sliced basil.

TIME 1 HOUR 30 MINUTES • SERVES 4

You've got a big crowd to feed and you want to do it in the quickest and most entertaining way. Instead of making individual pizzas, make a giant one. The only limits are the size of your pizza pan and the size of your oven. The kids can make the dough, roll it out and decorate it. The adults can supervise the baking process—the oven must be as hot as you can get it, which means turning it up to maximum for 15 minutes before you put in the pizza. Then everyone can get on with the eating.

I suggest a topping of tomato, cheese, basil and sausage, but it's up to your imagination and your kids' taste. If they insist on pineapple ... well, at least it's fruit. Make sure you use *fior de latte*—what we call cow's milk mozzarella.

2. Pizza di famiglia
The big pizza

500 g (1 lb) flour
20 g (¾ oz) fresh yeast
3 tbsp olive oil

FOR THE TOPPING
4 large tomatoes (or 400 g/13 oz
   tinned tomatoes)
100 g (3½ oz) *fior di latte* cheese,
   sliced
2 pork sausages, skinned and
   chopped
3 basil leaves
2 tbsp olive oil

Make the dough as described in the Calzone recipe on page 41, but add the 3 tablespoons of olive oil after you have mixed the warm water into the flour and yeast. After it has rested for at least 1 hour, work it again and roll it out to a thickness of about 1 cm (½ inch). Make a disc as large as the metal base on which you are going to bake the pizza. Preheat the oven to 240°C (475°F/gas 8); once it has reached that temperature, leave it for 15 minutes before putting in the pizza.

Thinly slice the tomatoes and spread the slices over the pizza base; alternatively, put the tinned tomatoes into a bowl and crush the pulp with your hands, then spread the pulp over the pizza base with a spoon. Scatter the *fior di latte* slices over the tomatoes, dot the pieces of sausages over and top with torn basil leaves. Pour a fine stream of olive oil over the pizza in a spiral from the centre.

Put the pizza into the preheated oven. After 2 minutes, turn the tray around 180 degrees. After another 5 minutes, use a fish slice to lift the base up and check if the bottom is turning golden—when it has, the pizza is ready.

TIME 1 HOUR 15 MINUTES • SERVES 4

Now you're familiar with working yeast, you can use it for a versatile batter. Talk about a hands-on activity. Let your kids help—they can stir, slap and splash it. This mixture is such fun to play with, you'll be amazed it can also turn into a meal. Just be prepared for a mess.

When frying zucchini flowers, try to use the male flower (the one attached to the vine) because it tastes better than the female flower (which is attached to the zucchini). You can follow the same process with sage leaves, but fry them for only 2 minutes. Or fry the batter by itself, a spoonful at a time, to make puffs that you sprinkle with sugar and cinnamon and serve with coffee. If you have any batter left, you can turn it into pizza dough by adding more flour and a few spoonfuls of olive oil. Keep adding flour until you have a wet dough, then follow the kneading and resting instructions for the Calzone recipe on page 41.

3. Fiori fritti
Fried zucchini flowers

15 g (½ oz) fresh yeast
400 g (13 oz) flour
8 zucchini flowers
olive oil for frying

In a large bowl, crumble the yeast into 3 cups of lukewarm water (at blood temperature). When it has dissolved, slowly add the flour, stirring and slapping it with your hands until the batter is smooth. You can tell that the yeast is activated when bubbles start to form spontaneously. Cover the bowl with a cloth and let it relax in a warm spot for 30 minutes.

Now the batter is ready for the zucchini flowers to be dipped and fried. Dip each zucchini flower into the batter, coating it thoroughly but thinly. Heat about 6 cm (2½ inches) of olive oil in a wok or deep frying pan until it sizzles when a little batter is thrown in. Fry the flowers until they are golden, about 3 minutes. Drain on paper towels before serving.

TIME 40 MINUTES • SERVES 4

This is a summer salad that uses *fior di latte* cheese (cow's milk mozzarella). Place it in the middle of a big table so your family and guests can help themselves. Ideally, make this in mid or late summer when tomatoes are at their best.

4. Insalata di mozzarella estiva
Fior di latte cheese with capsicum

2 red capsicums
1 bunch spring onions, trimmed
4 tbsp extra virgin olive oil
3 large tomatoes, chopped
120 g (4 oz) *fior di latte* cheese,
   cut into 8 thick slices
8 basil leaves, roughly chopped
1 tbsp balsamic vinegar
salt and freshly ground black
   pepper

Cut the capsicums in half, remove the seeds and cut them into long strips. Cut the spring onions in half lengthways. Put the capsicums and spring onions in a bowl, sprinkle with salt and pepper and pour on 2 tablespoons of extra virgin olive oil. Toss well.

Heat the barbecue or grill. When it's ready, grill the capsicums and onions for 5 minutes. Put them back in the bowl and add the chopped tomatoes. Mix well.

Arrange the slices of *fior di latte* along the centre of a serving platter. Heap the tomato–capsicum mixture over the slices and top with the chopped basil. Sprinkle over the balsamic vinegar and drizzle with the remaining extra virgin olive oil.

TIME 10 MINUTES • SERVES 4

The next two recipes are about eating outdoors, which can happen most of the year in this part of the world. But, of course, this food is good enough to be eaten indoors—and in any weather.

It's not essential to have a barbecue for the cooking—there's nothing wrong with an oven turned up high—and it's not essential to have a garden for the eating—nothing wrong with a big table and an open window. But it all works best if you have family and friends around to share the work and the pleasure.

5. Insalata di arance sanguinelle
Blood orange salad

6 blood oranges
1 clove garlic, finely chopped
1 tsp balsamic vinegar
2 tbsp extra virgin olive oil
1 tbsp finely chopped chives
salt and freshly ground black
    pepper

Peel the oranges, slicing off all the white pith and discarding it. Remove the segments from the connecting membranes. Place the orange segments in a salad bowl and squeeze over the juice remaining in the membranes with your hands. Mix together the garlic, balsamic vinegar and extra virgin olive oil and pour over the oranges. Season with salt and pepper and stir together gently. Leave to marinate for 10 minutes and serve on small plates, sprinkled with the chives.

TIME 15 MINUTES ● SERVES 4

Provola cheese is strong enough to stand up to grilling, and it has a flavour and texture that's meaty. It's great with these baked eggs. Serve them with crusty bread for dipping. You'll need about half a recipe of Napoletana sauce (but leave out the basil).

6. Uova con provola alla pizzaiola
Poached eggs with provola and spicy sauce

200 g (6½ oz) provola cheese
2 tsp dried oregano
250 ml (8 fl oz) Napoletana sauce
   (follow recipe, page 20, but
   leave out the basil)
4 eggs

4 x small copper pans or ramekins

Preheat the oven to 180°C (350°F/gas 4). Divide the provola into four equal slices and grill them—on the barbie, if you like—for 5 minutes on each side.

Stir the oregano into the sauce. Put 2 tablespoons of sauce in each ramekin. Put a slice of provola over the sauce, break an egg on top and pour more sauce around the egg. Bake the eggs in the preheated oven for 5 minutes, or a little longer if the egg whites don't seem to have set.

TIME 20 MINUTES • SERVES 4

In my home town of Naples there are shops that specialise in making potato croquettes, which in our dialect are known as *panzarotti*. They are a favourite after-school food and I often walked along the street with a paper cone full of *crocchette* munching these light, crisp treats.

7. Crocchette
Potato croquettes

5 medium potatoes, cleaned, with
   skin on
2 tbsp freshly grated parmesan
   cheese
1 tbsp butter
1 tbsp chopped parsley
2 eggs, separated
2 tbsp flour
3 tbsp dry breadcrumbs
olive oil or vegetable oil for frying
salt and freshly ground black
   pepper

Cook the potatoes in boiling water until tender, about 15 minutes. Drain, cool, peel and mash. Mix with the parmesan, butter, parsley, egg yolks, salt and pepper.

Shape the mixture into rectangles about 4 cm long and 2 cm tall (1½ x ¾ inches). Roll in the flour. Beat the egg whites until they start to thicken. Dip the shaped potato mixture into the egg whites and then dust with the breadcrumbs.

Pour about 6 cm (2½ inches) of oil into a wok or deep frying pan, heat until it sizzles when a drop of water is thrown in and fry the croquettes until golden, about 5 minutes. Drain on paper towels and serve.

TIME 30 MINUTES • SERVES 4

The success of this salad all depends on the quality of the tomatoes, so it is not a good idea to try it in midwinter when tomatoes tend to be hard, flavourless little objects out of hothouses. Serve it with focaccia. You could also serve this with these *involtini* of prosciutto and ricotta.

8. Pomodoro con pere al balsamico
Tomato and pear salad with prosciutto rolls

2 green pears (fairly hard), peeled
1 tsp balsamic vinegar
4 oxheart or other large tomatoes
extra virgin olive oil for serving
4 basil leaves, finely chopped
salt and freshly ground black
    pepper

FOR THE INVOLTINI
200 g (6½ oz) ricotta cheese
1 tbsp finely chopped chives
8 wide slices of prosciutto
salt and freshly ground black
    pepper

Finely grate the pears using a cheese grater. Mix them in a bowl with the balsamic vinegar and a little salt and pepper. Slice the tomatoes in discs, fan the slices out on a serving plate and sprinkle generously with salt. Spoon the pear and balsamic mixture over the tomatoes and splash over extra virgin olive oil. Sprinkle with a little basil.

To make the *involtini*, put the ricotta in a bowl and stir through it the chopped chives and a little salt and pepper. Lay out the slices of prosciutto and spread a tablespoon of the ricotta across one end of each slice. Roll up the prosciutto into cylinders about 2 cm (¾ inch) across.

TIME 15 MINUTES • SERVES 4

Broccoli is the healthiest of greens—a cancer fighter, among other qualities—and the best way to convince your kids to eat it is to serve it with cream. They can cope with just a little cholesterol occasionally.

9. Puré di broccoli
Broccoli puree

500 g (1 lb) broccoli, stalks
    removed
125 ml (4 fl oz) chicken stock
100 ml (3½ fl oz) cream
½ cauliflower, divided into florets
2 cloves garlic, sliced
1 small red chilli, finely sliced
3 tbsp olive oil
60 g (2 oz) pine nuts
salt

Break the broccoli heads into small pieces, throw them into a large saucepan of boiling water and simmer for 5 minutes. Drain and put the broccoli in a saucepan with the chicken stock. Cook uncovered over medium heat until the stock is absorbed by the broccoli and reduced by three-quarters, about 15 minutes. Lower the heat, pour in the cream and let the soup gently reduce and thicken for about 20 minutes, then puree it in a blender. Return to the saucepan and add salt to taste. Keep warm.

Meanwhile, cook the cauliflower florets in a saucepan of boiling water for about 10 minutes. In a large frying pan, sauté the garlic and chilli in the olive oil until the garlic turns golden, about 2 minutes. Add the drained cauliflower, toss and cook for another 5 minutes, turning often.

Dry-roast the pine nuts: heat a heavy-based frying pan, add the pine nuts and toss until golden (watch them to make sure they don't burn).

Divide the hot broccoli puree between four bowls, top with pieces of cauliflower, sprinkle with the pine nuts and serve immediately.

TIME 45 MINUTES   ●   SERVES 4

Here's a light and healthy soup that will hold the kids' attention because it is served with parmesan. This recipe, minus the fennel, is also the basic way of making chicken stock.

10. Brodo di pollo
Chicken broth with fennel

1 x 1.5 kg (3 lb) chicken
2 carrots, roughly chopped
1 stick celery, roughly chopped
2 onions, roughly chopped
10 sprigs of parsley, leaves and
    stems roughly chopped
2 tbsp olive oil
2 fennel bulbs
100 g (3½ oz) freshly grated
    parmesan cheese
1 tbsp finely chopped parsley
salt and freshly ground black
    pepper

Cut the legs off the chicken. Split the carcass in half lengthways, then cut each in half crossways. Place the carrots, celery and onions in a large saucepan with the roughly chopped parsley leaves and stems and 1 tablespoon of the olive oil. Cook over low heat for 10 minutes. Add the chicken pieces and toss for 2 minutes. Pour over enough cold water to completely cover the chicken, bring to a boil and simmer gently, uncovered, for 1 hour.

Strain the liquid into another saucepan, reserving the chicken pieces and discarding the vegetables. Remove the skin from the chicken, shred the meat and set it aside. Cut the tops off the fennel bulbs, slice the fennel in half lengthways, then cut out and discard the core at the bottom; cut in half again.

Add the fennel pieces to the stock in the saucepan and cook for 20 minutes uncovered. Add the shredded chicken and cook for a few more minutes until the meat is heated through. Season to taste.

Serve the *brodo* in individual bowls sprinkled with parmesan cheese and the finely chopped parsley.

TIME 1 HOUR 30 MINUTES • SERVES 4

Now we come to what we Italians call *cucina povera*—historically, the cooking of the poor, but now a highly fashionable style with the rich, who have noticed that the poor often eat well and stay healthy.

The next four dishes are variants on pasta *in brodo* (see recipe, page 53)—they're too thick to be soup, but too wet to be considered pasta with sauce. The idea is that you use any dried pasta you have in the cupboard, including all the broken bits at the bottom of your pasta packets. So though I've named pasta shapes in the list of ingredients, you can substitute any other types you prefer. And I like to eat the peas when they're in season, in spring and early summer.

This is casual eating—food of the trattoria not the ristorante, unless the ristorante has discovered the appeal of *cucina povera*. These are dishes you can eat with a fork but need to finish with a spoon or a wipe of bread. They are all enough for four as a first course. If you want to serve them as main dishes, double the quantities.

11. Quattro piccole paste
Four little pastas

Pasta e fagioli (Pasta with beans)

100 g (3½ oz) dried cannellini
   beans
2 medium onions, chopped
2 tbsp olive oil
1 medium carrot, chopped
1 stalk celery, chopped
1 tomato, chopped
2 cloves garlic, peeled
200 g (6½ oz) *tubetti* pasta
45 g (1½ oz) freshly grated
   parmesan cheese
1 tbsp finely chopped parsley
extra virgin olive oil for serving
salt

Soak the beans for at least 6 hours in a saucepan of water. Drain and replace the water, bring the beans to a boil, then reduce the heat and simmer until they are soft, about 45 minutes. Strain the beans, keeping the cooking liquid.

In a saucepan, sauté the onions in the olive oil for 10 minutes, then add the carrot and celery and cook for another 5 minutes. Add the beans, tomato and garlic and sauté for 2 minutes, then add 250 ml (8 fl oz) of the reserved bean cooking liquid. Bring to the boil, then turn off the heat. Remove and discard the garlic.

Meanwhile, add salt to a large saucepan of boiling water, put in the *tubetti* pasta and cook for 5 minutes. Strain, discarding the water. Add the pasta to the soup, turn on the heat and simmer for 3 more minutes. If it seems too dry, add another cup of the bean water. Season to taste.

Serve sprinkled with parmesan cheese and parsley and drizzle over some extra virgin olive oil.

TIME 7 HOURS, INCLUDING SOAKING • SERVES 4 AS FIRST COURSE

RECIPES CONTINUE ON PAGE 56

Pasta e patate (Pasta with potato)

2 large potatoes, peeled and cut
    into small cubes
1 onion, finely chopped
3 tbsp olive oil
500 ml (16 fl oz) chicken stock
4 tbsp tomato puree
250 g (8 oz) linguine or spaghetti,
    broken into small pieces
4 tbsp freshly grated parmesan
    cheese, plus extra for serving
salt and freshly ground black
    pepper

Wash the cubes of potato several times in cold water to reduce starch, then drain. Put the chopped onion into a saucepan with the olive oil and sauté over medium heat for 5 minutes. Add the potatoes and cook for another 3 minutes, stirring. Pour in the chicken stock, bring to the boil and simmer. After 10 minutes, add the tomato puree and continue simmering for another 10 minutes.

Add the pasta and cook until it is *al dente*, about 7 minutes. If the mixture seems to be drying out, add 125 ml (4 fl oz) of hot water. Add the grated parmesan and stir it through. Turn off the heat and let the pasta relax for 1 minute. Add salt and pepper to your taste. Serve with more parmesan.

TIME 40 MINUTES • SERVES 4 AS FIRST COURSE

Pasta e piselli (Pasta and peas)

1 small onion, finely chopped
4 tbsp olive oil
75 g (2½ oz) pancetta (or bacon),
    diced
150 g (5 oz) shelled fresh peas
1 litre (35 fl oz) chicken stock
    (or water)
200 g (6½ oz) *tubetti* pasta
4 tbsp freshly grated parmesan
    cheese
salt and freshly ground black
    pepper

Put the onion and olive oil into a heavy-based saucepan. Cook over medium heat for 10 minutes, stirring often. Add the pancetta, and when it is sizzling add the peas. Sauté for 3 minutes, then add the stock. Bring to the boil and simmer, uncovered, for 10 minutes.

Meanwhile, add salt to a large saucepan of boiling water, put in the pasta and cook for 5 minutes (it should be undercooked). Drain and add to the pea and onion mixture. Simmer for another 3 minutes. Season with salt and pepper to your taste.

Divide among four plates and serve sprinkled with parmesan cheese.

TIME 30 MINUTES • SERVES 4 AS FIRST COURSE

Pasta con ceci (Pasta with chickpeas)

150 g (5 oz) dried chickpeas
2 cloves garlic, peeled
2 tbsp olive oil
1 tomato, chopped
leaves of 3 stems rosemary
250 g (8 oz) pappardelle, broken
   into small pieces
extra virgin olive oil for serving
salt and freshly ground black
   pepper

Soak the chickpeas for at least 6 hours in a saucepan of water. Drain and replace the water, bring the chickpeas to the boil and simmer until they are soft, about 1 hour. Skim off any froth. Strain the chickpeas but retain the cooking liquid.

In a large saucepan, sauté the garlic cloves in the olive oil until golden, about 2 minutes. Add the chickpeas and cook for 2 minutes. Add the tomato and cook for a further 2 minutes, then add the chickpea cooking water and the leaves from 2 stems of rosemary. Bring to the boil and discard the garlic. Add the broken pappardelle and bring to the boil again. Turn off the heat and allow to sit for 20 minutes.

When you're ready to serve, warm the soup up again, finely chop the remaining rosemary leaves and sprinkle over the top. Season to taste. Serve in four plates and drizzle extra virgin olive oil over each.

TIME 8 HOURS, INCLUDING SOAKING • SERVES 4 AS FIRST COURSE

For some reason, the fish we call San Pietro (Saint Peter) in Italian is called John Dory in English. Italian fishermen tell the story that the black circle found on the fish's skin is the thumbprint of the original Christian fisherman, Peter. Presumably English and Australian fishermen say it's the thumb of Saint John. Whatever the name, the flavour is fine. Cooked in parmesan batter with mashed peas and a cream sauce, it is a favourite with all our family.

12. San Pietro con crema di piselli

John Dory with pea puree

4 eggs
50 g (1¾ oz) freshly grated
    parmesan cheese
1 tbsp finely chopped parsley
olive oil for frying
4 x 180 g (6 oz) John Dory fillets,
    each sliced into 3 long pieces
100 g (3½ oz) flour
salt and freshly ground black
    pepper

FOR THE PUREE
250 g (8 oz) unshelled fresh peas
100 g (3½ oz) shallots, finely
    chopped
50 g (1¾ oz) butter
150 ml (5 fl oz) dry white wine
150 ml (5 fl oz) cream
salt and freshly ground black
    pepper

FOR THE SAUCE
50 g (1¾ oz) unsalted butter
100 ml (3½ fl oz) cream

To make the puree, shell the peas and boil them in plenty of water for about 10 minutes. Drain. Put the shallots in a saucepan with the butter and sauté over medium heat until golden, about 5 minutes. Add the peas, lower the heat and stir for 2 minutes. Add the wine and simmer until most of the wine has disappeared, about 10 minutes.

Put the peas into a blender and blend until the mixture is smooth. Pour it into a saucepan, add the cream and salt and pepper to taste, and stir thoroughly over low heat until the mixture is thick, about 5 minutes. Set aside.

Make the coating for the fish. In a shallow bowl beat the eggs until creamy, add the parmesan and beat again. Stir in half the chopped parsley and season with salt and pepper. Heat about 6 cm (2½ inches) of olive oil in a wok or deep frying pan until it sizzles when a drop of water is thrown in. Dust each piece of fish in the flour, shaking off any excess, then dip into the egg mix. Gently put the fish fillets into the hot oil and fry until golden, about 3 minutes. Drain the fish on paper towels.

For the sauce, melt the unsalted butter in a frying pan over medium heat and sizzle until it turns golden brown, about 2 minutes—watch carefully so it doesn't burn. Add the cream and cook over low heat until the sauce becomes thick, about 5 minutes. Add the remaining finely chopped parsley and stir.

To serve, warm the pea puree and divide it among four plates. On each plate place three pieces of fish on top of the peas and pour a few teaspoons of sauce over each piece of fish just before serving.

TIME 45 MINUTES • SERVES 4

The most important thing to remember when you're barbecuing seafood is to allow different times for different creatures so they don't become dry and tough. Serve them with a tomato salad sprinkled with dried oregano. I've suggested some ingredients here, but you can substitute others.

13. Grigliata mista di mare
Seafood barbecue

4 small calamari, cleaned
1 medium octopus, cleaned and
    roughly chopped
4 sand whiting, scaled and gutted
2 slices tuna or swordfish, each
    about 2 cm (¾ inch) thick
8 green medium prawns, in shells
4 sardines, gutted
125 ml (4 fl oz) olive oil
250 ml (8 fl oz) extra virgin olive oil
3 tbsp finely chopped parsley
juice of 1 lemon

Cook the calamari and the octopus in a saucepan of boiling water for 10 minutes, then drain. Toss all the seafood in olive oil so they are well coated. Barbecue all (except the prawns) on a hot plate for 5 minutes, then add the prawns and continue cooking for a further 10 minutes. Then barbecue over an open flame for another 5 minutes.

Mix together the extra virgin olive oil, parsley and lemon juice, whisking to add air, pour over the seafood and serve.

TIME 35 MINUTES • SERVES 4

The grilled T-bone is a Tuscan classic. Italians tend to like their beef well done (*ben cotta*) rather than rare (*al sangue*). That's because the *chianina* cattle of Tuscany are fatter than the cattle raised in most countries. The fat in this cut makes the meat very tasty, which is why Italians very rarely serve sauce on their beef. With leaner T-bones, we need to add a bit of flavour, like this sauce.

Personally, I think the T-bone is best cooked just on the rare side of medium (about 5 minutes on each side), but if you've eaten your meat well done all your life, don't listen to me.

14. Bistecca Fiorentina all'Armando
T-bone steak, my way

4 x 500 g (1 lb) T-bone steaks
3 tbsp olive oil
1 tsp finely chopped garlic
125 ml (4 fl oz) beef stock
2 tbsp balsamic vinegar
4 handfuls rocket leaves, coarsely
   chopped
sea salt and freshly ground black
   pepper

Put the T-bones on a preheated hot plate or pan (or over the flames of the barbecue if you like a more charcoal taste). Grind over a lot of black pepper and cook them to the taste of each guest.

While the meat is grilling, put the olive oil and garlic in a frying pan and sizzle the garlic until it's golden, about 1 minute. Add the beef stock and balsamic vinegar, bring to the boil and then reduce for about 1 minute. Taste to see if it needs salt.

Place a T-bone on each plate, splash over the sauce and place some chopped rocket on the side.

TIME 15 MINUTES • SERVES 4

This is another straightforward barbecue mixture. But the secret is to put the meat in the marinade the night before. The lamb and quails get a rosemary marinade, and the pork is marinated in a honey mixture. Serve with a rocket salad.

15. Grigliata mista di carne
Mixed grill

4 lamb chops
2 quails, butterflied
2 pork chops
4 Italian pork sausages

FOR THE LAMB AND QUAIL
    MARINADE
1 clove garlic, crushed
leaves of 3 stems rosemary
125 ml (4 fl oz) extra virgin olive oil

FOR THE PORK MARINADE
2 tbsp honey
125 ml (4 fl oz) extra virgin olive oil
125 ml (4 fl oz) white wine
1 garlic clove, crushed
leaves of 5 sprigs thyme

For the lamb and quail marinade, mix together the garlic, rosemary and extra virgin olive oil. Rub the marinade all over the lamb and quails and marinate overnight. For the pork marinade, mix together the honey, extra virgin olive oil, white wine, garlic and thyme leaves. Rub all over the chops and let them marinate for at least 12 hours.

Heat the hot plate of your barbecue. Put on the sausages first, then after 5 minutes add the pork, and after another 5 minutes the lamb and quails. Continue cooking until all the meat is done. The aim is to have the sausages and pork well done and the lamb and quails medium.

TIME 12 HOURS 30 MINUTES, INCLUDING MARINATING • SERVES 4

Here's another favourite I've been making since I arrived in Australia, the land of barbecue. The ingredients include a clean house brick, which you should not attempt to eat. It's there to seal in the flavour. The dish's Italian name suggests that it is the devil's spatchcock. I like to say it's been through hell in the cooking but tastes like heaven. You need to start the recipe the night before you plan to serve it.

16. Galletto alla diavola
Peppered spatchcock

8 medium-sized spatchcocks
juice of 8 lemons
freshly ground black pepper

FOR THE MARINADE
500 ml (16 fl oz) white wine
3 tbsp olive oil
3 bay leaves
pinch of salt

1 x clean house brick (or other
   heavy object)

Cut each spatchcock in half lengthways and marinate for at least 12 hours in the mixture of the wine, olive oil, bay leaves and salt.

Heat the hot plate of your barbecue or a heavy-based frying pan on top of your stove. When it is very hot, put in the spatchcock pieces, skin side up, and grind over a lot of black pepper. When you think you've ground enough pepper, grind on more.

Put the brick on top of the spatchock and cook for 15 minutes. Lift off the brick, turn the spatchcock over so the skin side is in contact with the hot plate or pan, grind on more pepper and put the brick back. Cook for another 15 minutes. Serve, skin side up, with lemon juice squeezed over.

TIME 12 HOURS 30 MINUTES, INCLUDING MARINATING • SERVES 4

On any Sunday the streets of Naples are fragrant with the smell of meat cooking slowly all morning to be ready for the long festive lunch. The recipe may vary a little from house to house, according to flavouring tricks passed down the female line over the centuries, but the purpose is the same: two or three generations get together around a table to fill their bellies and share their dreams.

Although *ragú* is often translated as 'meat sauce', it's really more of a stew served as two courses—first a pasta sauce made from the meat juices, and then tender pieces of beef or pork served with vegetables. I recommend roast or mashed potatoes and a big rocket salad (peppery enough to clean your palate). The *ragú* is often preceded by an appetiser of fried fish—usually small whiting, whitebait, cuttlefish, tiny prawns, all tossed in flour and deep-fried in olive oil for 5 minutes. In Naples most people are content to have some fruit as a dessert after all that.

I suggest you save a few cupfuls of the *ragú* sauce and freeze it for use in other recipes.

17. Ragú
The Sunday feast

400 g (13 oz) pork shoulder
400 g (13 oz) beef shoulder
1 onion, chopped
4 tbsp olive oil
2 bay leaves
2 cloves
185 ml (6 fl oz) red wine
250 g (8 oz) tomato paste
400 g (13 oz) tinned tomatoes
400 g (13 oz) rigatoni or other
    tube pasta
250 g (8 oz) ricotta cheese
freshly grated parmesan cheese
    for serving
salt and freshly ground black
    pepper

Chop the meats into large cubes, about 5 cm (2 inches) square. In a large casserole dish, sauté the onion in the olive oil for 10 minutes over medium heat. Turn up the heat, toss in the meat cubes and brown them on all sides, about 5 minutes. Add the bay leaves, cloves and red wine. Simmer uncovered until most of the red wine is evaporated, about 10 minutes. Add the tomato paste and the tomatoes.

Simmer uncovered over low heat for 3 hours, stirring regularly with a wooden spoon and checking every 20 minutes or so to see if the sauce is drying out—in which case, add 125 ml (4 fl oz) of water. When the *ragú* is cooked, the sauce will be very thick. Spoon most of the liquid into a separate saucepan to be used as the pasta sauce (but save several cups for use in other recipes—it can be frozen when it cools down). Put the lid on the casserole dish and put it back into a low oven to keep the meat warm for the main course.

Add salt to a large saucepan of boiling water, throw in the pasta and cook until *al dente*, about 8 minutes. Drain. Stir the ricotta through the meat sauce. Add the pasta and stir thoroughly. Season to taste and serve sprinkled with parmesan.

When you are ready for the main course, take the meat out of the oven and arrange on a serving plate.

TIME 3 HOURS 30 MINUTES • SERVES 4

Here's a classic Italian dish supposedly invented on the island of Capri, which we can see from the Bay of Naples. Many Italian restaurants outside Italy serve it, but some of them think they can get away with using cheap meat—yearling rather than true veal. *Caprese* is only worth cooking if the meat is meltingly tender, not tough. Serve this with roast potatoes and green beans.

18. Scaloppine alla caprese
Veal with eggplant

16 thin slices veal, each about 50 g (1½ oz)
100 g (3½ oz) flour
2 tbsp olive oil, plus extra for frying
2 medium eggplants, each cut crossways into 8 slices 5 mm (¼ inch) thick
16 slices of *fior di latte* cheese
16 basil leaves
1 tbsp butter
125 ml (4 fl oz) Napoletana sauce (see recipe, page 20)
60 ml (2 fl oz) dry white wine

Spread plastic wrap over the meat slices and gently beat them with a mallet or rolling pin until they spread out to about double their original size. Dip the pieces in flour, being careful to coat both sides. Heat the 2 tablespoons of olive oil in a frying pan over medium heat and sauté the veal for about 2 minutes on each side. Lay them in a clean frying pan in a single layer.

Pour olive oil into a wok or deep frying pan to a depth of about 6 cm (2½ inches), heat until it sizzles when a drop of water is thrown in, and fry the eggplant slices until they are golden, about 3 minutes. Drain them on paper towels.

Lay a slice of eggplant on each piece of veal, then a slice of *fior de latte*, and top with a basil leaf and a dab of butter. Pour the Napoletana sauce and wine around the scaloppine. Cook over low heat for 5 minutes, basting with the juices in the pan.

To serve, put four scaloppine on each plate. Reduce the remaining liquid in the pan over high heat for 1 minute and pour the sauce over the scaloppine.

TIME 40 MINUTES • SERVES 4

I'm calling this schnitzel, although strictly speaking this is a recipe for *costoletta milanese*, the crumbed veal chop for which Milan is justly famous. I'm combining it with a classic Naples vegetable dish—*parmigiana*, or eggplant with parmesan and basil. Because this is a meeting of northern and southern cooking I've given it an Italian name that honours the town of Teano, where King Vittorio Emmanuele, who was advancing from the north, met up with Giuseppe Garibaldi and his army moving from the south on 26 October 1860. The two leaders shook hands and finalised the unification of a bunch of warring city states into a nation called Italy.

Normally *parmigiana* is cooked and served in the same baking dish. But here each guest receives one veal chop and an elegant individual moulded cylinder of *parmigiana*.

19. Costoletta alla Teano
Schnitzel with eggplant parmigiana

FOR THE PARMIGIANA

3 large eggplants

flour for dusting

olive oil for frying

200 g (6½ oz) provola cheese

750 ml (24 fl oz) Napoletana sauce
    (see recipe, page 20)

200 g (6½ oz) freshly grated
    parmesan cheese

16 large basil leaves

FOR THE COSTOLETTA

4 thick veal cutlets, each about
    250 g (8 oz)

2 egg whites

flour for dusting

6 tbsp dry breadcrumbs

about 2 tbsp olive oil

about 2 tbsp butter

4 x metal moulds or ramekins,
    7 cm diameter x 6 cm deep
    (2¾ x 2½ inches)

Preheat the oven to 200°C (400°F/gas 6) and make the *parmigiana*. Cut the eggplants lengthways into slices about 1 cm (½ inch) thick. Then cut the slices into discs by pressing down with a circular mould (if you have one) or with the rim of a cup or ramekin. You should aim for five discs per person. Dust the eggplant with flour. Pour olive oil into a wok or deep frying pan to a depth of about 6 cm (2½ inches), heat until it sizzles when a drop of water is thrown in and fry the eggplant slices until they are golden. Drain on paper towels.

Cut the provola into 16 slices, each about 5 mm (¼ inch) thick and with a slightly smaller diameter than the eggplant. Cut out discs of greaseproof paper slightly larger than the metal mould or ramekin you are using. Put the greaseproof paper circles onto a baking tray and a mould on top of each. If you are using ramekins, there is no need to line them with paper; just place them on the baking tray.

Place one piece of eggplant at the base of the mould or ramekin, drizzle over a teaspoon of Napoletana sauce, then cover with a slice of provola. Add another teaspoon of sauce, a layer of grated parmesan and a basil leaf. Then add another layer of eggplant, followed by sauce, provola, sauce, parmesan, basil, eggplant, and so on, finishing with eggplant, a teaspoonful of sauce and a sprinkling of parmesan. You should end up with a stack of five eggplant slices with four layers of provola sandwiched between. Bake for about 12 minutes until the top is golden.

RECIPE CONTINUES ON PAGE 70

Prepare the *costoletta* before putting the *parmigiana* into the oven; they bake at the same time. Place each cutlet on a hard surface, such as a chopping board. With a small, sharp knife, slice partway along the bone, so that about two-thirds of the length of the meat is still attached. Put some plastic wrap over the cutlet and hammer it with a food mallet or other heavy object until the meat has spread out and is about half as thick. Make sure it does not separate entirely from the bone.

Beat the egg whites until they thicken and become translucent. Dip the cutlets in flour, then in the egg white, then in the breadcrumbs. Heat a tablespoon each of olive oil and butter in a frying pan until a breadcrumb thrown in sizzles: if the oil is lukewarm, the breadcrumbs will soak up too much of it, and it should not be so hot it's smoking. Put in the cutlets and turn down the flame. Sauté the cutlets for 2 minutes on each side until a crunchy crust is formed. Take them out of the pan and place on a baking tray. You'll have to do this in batches; add more butter and olive oil to the pan if you need to.

Put the *parmigiana* into the preheated oven. After 4 minutes, put in the *costoletta* (on a rack below the *parmigiana*) and bake for a further 8 minutes. Take the *parmigiana* out of the oven. Check the meat: most people like veal medium to well done, so take out one cutlet, make a small incision and check the colour of the meat. If it's still pink, put the cutlets back in the oven for another 2 minutes.

Let the *parmigiana* cylinders cool for a minute. Slide a fish slice under the mould, and lift it onto a serving plate. Using tongs, pull the greaseproof paper out from under the mould, then carefully lift the mould from around the stack of eggplants. If you are using ramekins, upend each one onto a plate. Then place a *costoletta* next to the *parmigiana* and serve.

TIME 1 HOUR 20 MINUTES • SERVES 4

Here's an elegant refreshment you can serve at lunch or as a palate cleanser between courses during a more elegant dinner. It's similar to a sorbet, only crunchy. To achieve this effect, the granita needs to be stirred up with a fork—not swirled in an ice-cream machine.

20. Granita di limo
Lime granita

250 g (8 oz) sugar
juice of 6 limes, about 200 ml
   (6½ fl oz)
juice of 1 lemon
1 tbsp chopped mint

In a saucepan, boil 1 litre (35 fl oz) of water, add the sugar and stir until it melts. Let the syrup cool, then add the lime and lemon juice.

Pour the liquid into a tub or large tray and put it into the freezer. After 15 minutes take the tray out and use a fork to break any ice that has formed up into small fragments. Put the tray back into the freezer. Repeat this process three times, about every 15 minutes. The idea is to prevent the granita from setting into a solid block; instead, it should be tiny crystals. Four stirrings should be enough. Leave it to finish freezing for at least 2 hours. Serve in long glasses with a little chopped mint on top.

VARIATION: You can make a melon granita by the same method. Simply puree the flesh of a sweet ripe melon (don't add any sugar) and freeze as before. If you serve the melon granita with a drop of orange blossom syrup (from Lebanese grocers), you have a sophisticated Middle Eastern treat.

TIME 3 HOURS 15 MINUTES, INCLUDING FREEZING • SERVES 4

You could call this a version of the fine Spanish drink sangria. Spain was in control of Naples for 300 years, so we're allowed to borrow from them—or even claim their food as our own. I suggest using a pinot noir. I find people like to eat the peach and drink the wine separately.

21. Pesche in vino rosso
Yellow peaches in red wine

4 ripe yellow peaches
1 litre (35 fl oz) light red wine

Peel the peaches and slice them into eighths. Put the slices in a jug with the red wine. Cover and place in the fridge for 2 hours before serving.

TIME 2 HOURS, INCLUDING MARINATING • SERVES 4

Most people don't have a gelato machine, so making ice-cream at home can be difficult. But there's a great alternative to ice-cream, used all over Italy—semifreddo, which literally translates as 'half-cold'. It requires no special equipment apart from your imagination. Gelato is based on milk. Semifreddo uses cream. The important principles are that the cream must be very fresh and you should beat it immediately before you plan to freeze it.

The flavourings are whatever takes your fantasy. As soon as the cream is whipped, you could add slices of nougat or small pieces of fruit or chocolate chips or whatever you like. Or you can fill a mould with layers of semifreddo in different colours, and layers of biscuit or sponge or dried or fresh fruits—or prunes and pistachio nuts, as here. If you are using liqueur as flavouring, apply it lightly—too much alcohol can interfere with the freezing process.

22. Semifreddo
Not quite ice-cream

24 prunes, pitted
½ lemon, roughly chopped
8 tbsp sugar
6 eggs, separated, from which you
    use 6 yolks and 3 whites
600 ml (19½ fl oz) cream
15 amaretti biscuits, crushed
100 ml (3½ fl oz) brandy
60 g (2 oz) unsalted pistachio nuts,
    shelled and crushed

Put the prunes, lemon pieces, 2 tablespoons of the sugar and 500 ml (16 fl oz) of water in a pan and simmer uncovered for 1 hour. Allow to cool. Drain the prunes, reserving the juice. Discard the pieces of lemon.

Thoroughly blend the 6 egg yolks with 4 tablespoons of sugar. Beat the cream until fairly stiff and fold it into the egg yolk mixture. In a clean bowl, whisk the 3 egg whites until they form stiff peaks. Gently fold them into the egg mixture. (That's the basic semifreddo, which can go straight into the freezer if you want to serve it plain.)

To flavour the semifreddo, fold in the amaretti, brandy and the pistachio nuts (reserving a few for decoration) and stir well. Line a deep rectangular container with greaseproof paper. Pour in about one-third of the mixture and spread it out evenly. Layer half the prunes over the semifreddo. Cover them with another third of the mixture, then the other half of the prunes, then the final third of the semifreddo mixture. Freeze for at least 4 hours.

About 15 minutes before you are ready to serve, put the prune juice into a saucepan with 2 cups of water and the remaining 2 tablespoons of sugar and simmer uncovered over a low heat until it thickens into a syrup, about 10 minutes. Allow to cool for a few minutes.

TIME 5 HOURS, INCLUDING FREEZING • SERVES 4

Most Italians grow up with the sound of their mothers whisking eggs and sugar together to make *zabaglione*, especially when they're recovering from an illness. It's a nourishing treat, often boosted with a shot of coffee or sweet alcohol. You can eat it as a dessert on its own, or pour it over fresh fruit (such as strawberries) in a cocktail glass. Here are two versions.

23. Zabaglione
Egg nog

8 egg yolks
4 tbsp sugar
a little cocoa, for children's version
2 demitasse cups warm espresso
    coffee (or 4 tbsp Marsala and
    2 tbsp brandy), for hot
    zabaglione

For the basic kids' version, put the egg yolks and sugar in a large bowl and whisk them together. It's ready when the mixture thickens and starts to bubble of its own accord—at least 15 minutes. Sprinkle a little cocoa on top and serve with savoiardi (sponge-finger) biscuits for dipping.

To serve the *zabaglione* hot, put the egg yolks and sugar in a large bowl and whisk for 10 minutes, then add the warm espresso coffee or the Marsala and brandy. Boil about 1 litre (35 fl oz) of water in a large saucepan, turn off the heat and place the mixing bowl over the hot water and continue to whisk. The idea is to gently warm the *zabaglione* so it becomes creamy without turning into scrambled eggs. Serve it in wide glasses with long spoons—with berries if you like.

TIME 20 MINUTES • SERVES 4

This was the first dessert created by my father and me when we opened Pulcinella in Sydney in 1979. Mascarpone is not just the cheese, but a whipped dessert with eggs, brandy and any liqueur that's to your taste. Serve it with fresh fruit and sweet biscuits for dipping.

24. Mascarpone
Cream cheese sundae

5 eggs, separated
5 tbsp caster sugar
500 g (1 lb) mascarpone cheese
60 ml (2 fl oz) brandy
60 ml (2 fl oz) Strega liqueur
    (or Galliano)

In a mixer, beat the egg yolks with the sugar, then blend in the mascarpone at high speed. Stir in the brandy and Strega. Whip the egg whites until stiff, then gently fold them into the mascarpone mixture. Refrigerate until ready to serve.

TIME 10 MINUTES • SERVES 4

This is not a soufflé, although it looks like one—for 30 years my customers have kept asking for 'that cherry soufflé thing you do'. It has more in common with a trifle or a cake, and it uses the marvellous mascarpone mixture opposite as well as soft, sweet savoiardi biscuits (named for the Savoy family, who were the first kings of the united Italy back in 1860).

The quantities in this recipe are enough for four small cherry cakes (for which you'll need soufflé dishes). And you can use tinned cherries rather than fresh ones—in fact, the tinned ones keep their flavour better after baking and you can find them all year round.

25. Torta mascarpone
Cherry cake

24 savoiardi (sponge-finger)
   biscuits
250 ml (8 fl oz) milk, warmed
60 ml (2 fl oz) Strega liqueur
   (or Galliano)
10 tbsp whipped mascarpone
   (see recipe #24, opposite)
200 g (6½ oz) tinned cherries,
   drained with syrup reserved
5 egg whites
pinch of salt
4 tsp sugar
icing sugar for dusting
vanilla ice-cream to serve (optional)

4 x soufflé dishes, 12 cm diameter x
   5 cm deep (5 x 2 inches)

Preheat the oven to 200°C (400°F/gas 6). For each cake, dip three biscuits quickly in the warmed milk and lay them in a soufflé dish. Using a brush, paint the top of the biscuits with a little Strega. Top with 1 tablespoon of whipped mascarpone and 3 or 4 cherries, and cover with a teaspoon of the cherry syrup. Dip three more biscuits in milk, and create another layer of mascarpone, cherries and syrup.

Beat the egg whites with the salt until stiff. Spoon a quarter of the egg white mixture into each soufflé dish so that it projects about 1 cm (½ inch) above the rim. Sprinkle each with 1 teaspoon of sugar. Bake in the preheated oven until the tops are golden, about 7 minutes.

To serve, dust with icing sugar. You can make a hole in the centre of each souffle and put in a tablespoon of vanilla ice-cream.

TIME 25 MINUTES • SERVES 4

3

traditions
and twists

Some people are under the impression that Italian food has been the same forever, and that our 'standard' dishes are fixed and immutable. In fact, what we call the classics these days were once radical innovations.

Italian cooking has been evolving over the centuries, as it constantly adapts to welcome the arrival of new produce from other countries and cultures. Very few of our favourite ingredients originated in the European peninsula that reaches out towards Sicily.

Although garlic seems to have first appeared near what is now Naples five thousand years ago, we didn't have olive oil to cook it in until the Greeks brought it to us two millennia later. The Egyptians gave us wheat, from which the Romans and Etruscans were making fresh pasta around two thousand years ago (forget the nonsense about Marco Polo discovering it in China in the thirteenth century). Then, about the year 1000, the Arabs gave us the idea of drying strings of pasta to make portable food. And the Arabs introduced us to most of the herbs and spices we now take for granted.

Neapolitans were using wheat to make pizza bases two thousand years ago. Back then, pizza toppings would have included onions, cheese, anchovies and lentils. The tomato, regarded nowadays as an irreplaceable element of Italian cooking, didn't arrive in Europe until the sixteenth century—and was embraced by the Italians a hundred years before it was cautiously nibbled by the English (who never miss an opportunity to miss an opportunity when it comes to eating).

In the 1600s, around the same time as the tomato hit us, we got chillies, potatoes and corn (maize), which we started grinding to make polenta. Italians have gratefully absorbed all these elements into our home repertoire. Our cooking has always been *nuova cucina* (what others may call *nouvelle cuisine*) and every village—indeed every household—adds its own individual twists.

Here are my favourite interpretations of some of the classic dishes I grew up with. I see no point in repeating the clichés, so you won't find spaghetti bolognese here, or pesto or lemon gelato or chicken cacciatore. There are plenty of books about them.

What you will find are the modest re-imaginings of dishes you may not know so well but which deserve a continued life. Once you've tried them, I hope you'll be encouraged to make your own adaptations.

1. **Burrata con pomodori dolci** Cream cheese with candied tomatoes and basil sauce

2. **Zuppa di fagioli con cozze** Mussel and bean soup

3. **Crudo di pesce spada** Sliced swordfish with blood orange

4. **Carciofi ripieni** Stuffed globe artichokes

5. **Linguine all'amalfitana** Linguine with prawns and zucchini

6. **Maccheroni quattro formaggi** Macaroni four cheeses

7. **Gnocchi con salsa di vitello** Potato dumplings with veal *ragú*

8. **Arancini** Rice balls stuffed with chicken livers and mozzarella

9. **Verzi e risi** Rice with bacon and cabbage

10. **Zuppa di pesce** Fish stew

11. **Ricciola acqua pazza** Trevalla with cherry tomato sauce

12. **Trippa alla veronese** Tripe, Verona style

13. **Quaglie con peperoni** Baked quails stuffed with yellow capsicum

14. **Filetto alla marjorana** Beef with marjoram

15. **Braciolette napoletana** Rolled veal with pine nuts and raisins

16. **Braciolette Reginaldo** Veal rolls, Reg style

17. **Ossobuco alla genovese** Beef shanks with Marsala

18. **Coniglio alla Valleyfield** Rabbit, home style

19. **Torta di rabarbaro** Rhubarb tart

20. **Involtini di melanzane con ricotta e cioccolato** Chocolate eggplant

21. **Pastiera** Wheat and ricotta pie

22. **Tiramisu con fichi** Fig and mascarpone tart

23. **Semifreddo al torrone** Nougat semifreddo

24. **Zuccotto** Chocolate and ricotta dome cake

Burrata, which literally translates as 'buttered', is a form of creamy buffalo milk cheese that is imported from the Puglia region in southern Italy. If your local cheese shop doesn't stock it, urge them to get with the program and meanwhile grumpily substitute a creamy mozzarella.

Mozzarella, tomato and basil are the core ingredients of the classic *insalata caprese* but I like to serve *burrata* with a basil sauce and candied tomatoes, which is an idea I got from the Japanese. When you reflect that the tomato is technically a fruit, not a vegetable, you could try offering this as a dessert.

1. Burrata con pomodori dolci
Cream cheese with candied tomatoes and basil sauce

500 ml (16 fl oz) extra virgin
   olive oil
7 tbsp icing sugar
4 vine-ripened tomatoes, peeled
   and left whole
4 tbsp sugar
40 basil leaves
450 g (14 oz) *burrata* cheese
   (or fresh mozzarella)
salt

Mix together the olive oil and icing sugar in a bowl and put in the tomatoes. Leave to marinate for 12 hours. Pick out the tomatoes, and pat them dry with a paper towel. Coat in the 4 tablespoons of granular sugar. Place the tomatoes in a covered container and leave for another 6 hours.

Drain the liquid that has come off the tomatoes into a blender jar. Add the basil leaves, 1 tablespoon of oil from the marinade and a little salt. Blend into a sauce that is similar in texture to pesto.

Cut the *burrata* into four. Put a slice on each plate with a candied tomato next to it. Pour the basil sauce between the *burrata* and tomato—now you have the colours of the Italian flag—and serve.

TIME 18 HOURS, INCLUDING MARINATING • SERVES 4

Bean soup is a winter favourite in Italy and it's usually considered a dish from the mountains, where seafood is not exactly common. In Naples we've experimented—successfully I think— with the addition of mussels, which help to lighten the dish. The key here is not to overcook the mussels. They are added to the beans at the last possible minute.

2. Zuppa di fagioli con cozze
Mussel and bean soup

200 g (6½ oz) dried cannellini
   beans
1 medium onion, chopped
3 tbsp olive oil
1 medium carrot, chopped
½ stick celery, diced
4 tomatoes, diced
2 tsp dried oregano
40 mussels

Soak the cannellini beans in a large saucepan for at least 6 hours. Drain and replace the water. Boil the beans for 45 minutes. Let them cool down in their cooking liquid.

In a large saucepan, sauté the onion in the oil for 5 minutes, then add the carrot and celery and cook for another 5 minutes. Add the beans, all their cooking liquid and the tomatoes; simmer for 20 minutes. Stir in the oregano.

Scrub the mussels and snip off any protruding beards. In a separate saucepan, steam the mussels with a little water, with the lid on, over high heat for 2 minutes. Take the mussels out of the pan, remove them from their shells and add to the bean soup. Strain the mussel liquid through muslin to remove any grit and add it to the soup. Serve immediately.

TIME 7 HOURS 30 MINUTES, INCLUDING SOAKING • SERVES 4

A lot of restaurants offer 'seafood *carpaccio*' but, strictly speaking, the term *carpaccio* should apply only to finely sliced raw beef. In Naples the traditional term for marinated raw seafood is *crudo*, a dish we were enjoying long before the world discovered sushi. I've improved the look of the dish with segments of blood orange in a spiral pattern. When it's not blood orange season, you could use small pieces of grapefruit or a regular orange.

3. Crudo di pesce spada
Sliced swordfish with blood orange

1 clove garlic, peeled and flattened
100 ml (3½ fl oz) extra virgin olive
  oil
200 g (6½ oz) swordfish, eye fillet
  only
100 ml (3½ fl oz) lemon juice
4 blood oranges
1 tbsp finely chopped chives
salt
freshly cracked black pepper

FOR THE CANDIED ORANGE PEEL
1 large orange of strong colour
250 g (8 oz) sugar

Place the garlic in the olive oil and leave for 1 hour to flavour the oil. Discard the garlic.

Make the candied orange peel. Using a potato peeler, peel the skin off the orange. Eat the interior (or use it for another recipe). Cut the skin into long thin strips. Put the strips in a small saucepan, cover them with cold water, and bring to the boil. After 1 minute, strain. Put the orange skin back into the saucepan, cover with cold water, bring to the boil again and after 1 minute strain them. This process reduces bitterness. Now put the strips back into the saucepan with the sugar and 250 ml (8 fl oz) of water. Bring to the boil, then reduce the heat and simmer until the peel becomes translucent, about 10 minutes. Strain the strips and use them to decorate the fish.

Thinly slice the swordfish and arrange the slices flat on four serving plates. Squeeze the lemon juice over the fish and leave for 5 minutes. Remove excess lemon juice with a paper towel. Season with salt and freshly cracked pepper. Dress with the garlic-infused olive oil, spreading the oil evenly over the fish.

Peel the blood oranges, slicing off all the white pith, and remove the segments from the connecting membranes. Discard the skin.

To serve, arrange the blood orange segments in a spiral pattern in the centre of the dish and sprinkle the chives and the candied orange peel over the fish.

TIME 1 HOUR 10 MINUTES • SERVES 4

The standard version of this dish includes breadcrumbs and loads of cheese. I've lightened it so you can taste the nuttiness of the globe artichoke and you'll have room for a main course afterwards. I include the artichoke stems—they taste great and it is silly to throw them out. Be careful about drinking wine with this: there's a chemical in artichokes that neutralises the flavour of most whites. Drink a little rosé or pinot noir instead, and keep your vintage bottles for the next course.

4. Carciofi ripieni
Stuffed globe artichokes

8 globe artichokes
juice of 2 lemons
2 cloves garlic, sliced
400 ml (13 fl oz) white wine
20 ml (¾ fl oz) olive oil
parmesan cheese for serving
salt and freshly ground black
 pepper

FOR THE FILLING
8 tbsp finely chopped parsley
100 g (3½ oz) capers, chopped
120 g (4 oz) black olives, pitted
 and chopped
1 clove garlic, chopped
50 ml (1¾ fl oz) olive oil
salt and freshly ground black
 pepper

Preheat the oven to 200°C (400°F/gas 6). Before preparing the artichokes, add the lemon juice to 1 litre (35 fl oz) of water in a bowl and set aside. Cut the stems from the artichokes. Peel the stems and place in the bowl of water. Pull off and discard the outer leaves from the artichoke until only the pale yellow layers of leaves remain. Slice the tops from the artichokes, about a third of the way down. Pull apart the leaves and scoop out from the centre the middle leaves and the hairy choke. Place the artichokes in the bowl of water to prevent browning.

For the filling, combine the parsley, capers, olives and chopped garlic in a bowl and add salt and pepper to taste. Pour in the olive oil and mix well. Gently push open the artichoke leaves and, using a teaspoon, fill with stuffing. You should have some left over.

Put the sliced garlic and white wine in a baking pan, add the artichokes and their stems, then cover with foil. Place in the preheated oven for 20 minutes (or 30 minutes if the artichokes are large).

Meanwhile, place the remaining filling in a frying pan with the olive oil and a couple of tablespoons of water, sprinkle over salt and pepper and cook for a few minutes until the sauce thickens.

To serve, place the artichokes and stems on four serving plates and pour over the sauce. Top each one with a few shavings of parmesan.

TIME 40 MINUTES • SERVES 4

My friend Don Alfonso has an exciting restaurant on the Amalfi coast near Naples, which is the source of inspiration for this dish. You may get a shock to see parmesan listed in the ingredients—it is not supposed to go on seafood pasta. In Naples we have a habit of using a little parmesan with spaghetti *alle vongole* (clams) when there is no tomato in the sauce. The parmesan boosts the flavour of the other ingredients without dominating them. Here I extend that theory to prawns.

This is a convenient dish because the sauce can be cooked in precisely the same time it takes to boil the linguine, which you then throw into the frying pan and toss with the sauce before serving.

5. Linguine all'amalfitana
Linguine with prawns and zucchini

150 g (5 oz) green school prawns, peeled
300 g (10 oz) linguine
4 small zucchini, diced
9 tbsp extra virgin olive oil
2 cloves garlic, finely chopped
10 mint leaves, coarsely chopped
100 g (3½ oz) freshly grated parmesan cheese

Cut the heads and tails off the prawns and peel them. If you have not been able to find small prawns, cut large ones into pieces about 2 cm (¾ inch) long.

Make sure you have the ingredients ready for the sauce before you start cooking the pasta because they take the same time to cook. Add salt to a large saucepan of boiling water and throw in the linguine.

In a frying pan, sauté the zucchini in the extra virgin olive oil over high heat for 4 minutes, then add the garlic and cook until it becomes golden, about another minute. Stir, then add the prawns, and cook until they turn pink, another 2 minutes.

Strain the pasta and add it to the zucchini in the frying pan. Add the mint leaves and the parmesan, stir for half a minute and it's ready to serve.

TIME 10 MINUTES • SERVES 4

I first served this dish in a restaurant in Naples when I was 16 years old at a time when nobody worried about how rich a recipe might be. It's a celebration of the diversity of Italian cheeses—even though I do include one foreign cheese, Gruyère, from just over the border in Switzerland—and the wicked joy of cream. You couldn't describe this as 'modern'—it's one of those classics that suits only one season.

6. Maccheroni quattro formaggi
Macaroni four cheeses

50 g (1¾ oz) Gruyère cheese
50 g (1¾ oz) provolone dolce cheese
50 g (1¾ oz) *fior di latte* cheese
300 g (10 oz) penne
50 ml (1¾ fl oz) cream
50 ml (1¾ fl oz) beef stock
50 g (1¾ oz) freshly grated parmesan cheese
salt and freshly ground black pepper

Preheat the oven to 200°C (400°F/gas 6). Cut the Gruyère, provolone and *fior di latte* cheeses into small cubes. Add salt to a large saucepan of boiling water and throw in the pasta, cook for about 7 minutes, then drain.

Put the cream, stock, the cubed cheeses, pasta, salt and pepper in a large bowl and mix thoroughly. Butter a baking dish and pour in the pasta mixture. Sprinkle over the grated parmesan and bake in the preheated oven for 10 minutes. There is no need for more parmesan when serving.

TIME 20 MINUTES • SERVES 4

There are many recipes for gnocchi in Italy. Some use semolina instead of potatoes. Some add eggs or spinach. In Naples we sometimes call gnocchi *strozzapreti*, meaning 'choke priests', because they are solid creations of potato, flour and water. Here I'm suggesting you finish off the priest with a hearty sauce of stewed veal.

7. Gnocchi con salsa di vitello
Potato dumplings with veal ragú

FOR THE SAUCE
1 small onion, diced
4 tbsp olive oil
1 carrot, diced
1 celery stick, diced
2 bay leaves, torn
300 g (10 oz) veal backstrap, diced
250 ml (8 fl oz) white wine
100 ml (3½ fl oz) tomato puree
500 ml (16 fl oz) beef stock

FOR THE GNOCCHI
4 potatoes
200 g (6½ oz) flour

To make the sauce, in a frying pan sauté the onion in the olive oil for 5 minutes over medium heat, then add the carrot, celery and bay leaves and cook for another 5 minutes. Add the veal, turn up the heat and sear the meat for 3 minutes, turning often. Add the white wine, turn the heat down to medium and let the alcohol evaporate for 3 minutes. Add the tomato puree and bring back to the boil, then pour in the beef stock. Simmer uncovered over low heat for 45 minutes, adding a little water if the sauce seems to be drying out. Discard the bay leaves.

To make the gnocchi, boil the potatoes with their skins on for 20 minutes. Strain off the water, allow the potatoes to cool a little and remove the skins. Mash them to a smooth paste. Make a ring of the flour on a benchtop and pile the mashed potato into the centre. Work the flour and potato together with your hands until it makes a firm dough. Take a handful of the dough and roll it out into a cylinder about as thick as a finger. Cut the cylinder into pieces about 2 cm (¾ inch) long. Make an indentation in each piece with your thumb.

When you're ready to serve the dish, add salt to a large saucepan of boiling water and toss in the gnocchi. Scoop them out with a slotted spoon after they have risen to the surface, about 1 minute.

To serve, divide the gnocchi among four bowls and pour the veal sauce over them.

TIME 1 HOUR 40 MINUTES • SERVES 4

The word *arancini* means oranges. In this dish it refers more to the colour than the shape of the rice balls—since they tend to be pear-shaped. In Naples *arancini* (also known as *suppli* or *sartù di riso*) are made in their most elaborate form for festive occasions. Simplified, they are great as finger food at a party, or made from leftovers for family snacks or school lunches. There's a lot of hands-on activity for the kids here, moulding the rice into any shapes their imaginations—and the laws of physics—will allow. The spectacular version is given first, and then I explain how to simplify the process.

This is a perfect way in which to use any leftover *ragú* sauce that you've stored in the freezer (see recipe, page 66). If you don't like chicken livers, you can substitute salami.

8. Arancini
Rice balls stuffed with chicken livers and mozzarella

2 small white onions, finely chopped
125 g (4¼ oz) butter
400 g (13 oz) arborio rice
2 litres (72 fl oz) chicken stock
6 tbsp olive oil
120 g (4 oz) chicken livers (or finely chopped salami)
100 g (3½ oz) freshly grated parmesan cheese, plus extra for serving
about 250 ml (8 fl oz) *ragú* sauce (see recipe, page 66)
200 g (6½ oz) shelled fresh peas
4 quails' eggs
120 g (4 oz) smoked provola cheese (or mozzarella), in small cubes
2 egg whites, beaten
200 g (6½ oz) flour
200 g (6½ oz) dry breadcrumbs
salt and freshly ground black pepper

In a large saucepan, gently sauté 1 chopped onion in the butter for about 5 minutes. Add the rice and stir through the onion, then pour in all the chicken stock. Bring it to the boil and simmer the rice, covered, for about 15 minutes until all the stock is absorbed. The rice should be softer than it would be in risotto so it can be easily moulded into shape. Set aside.

While the rice is cooking, put half of the remaining chopped onion and 2 tablespoons of the olive oil in a frying pan and sauté for 10 minutes. Cut the chicken livers into 1-cm (½-inch) cubes, add to the onion and cook for a further 6 minutes, stirring often. Stir the grated parmesan and 5 tablespoons of *ragú* sauce through the rice, and mix thoroughly.

Cook the peas in boiling water for 10 minutes. Drain. In another frying pan, sauté the remaining onion in the remaining olive oil for 8 minutes, add the peas, stir and cook for 4 minutes. Grind some fresh pepper over the peas and set aside. Boil the quails' eggs for 4 minutes. Let them cool a little, then remove the shells.

Now you are ready to make the *arancini*. Preheat the oven to 200°C (400°F/gas 6). Put 1 heaped tablespoon of the rice mixture into the palm of your hand, and make a half-sphere shape with a well in the middle of the mound. Put a quarter of the chicken liver mixture, a quarter of the peas, a quarter of the provola cheese and one quail's egg into the well in the middle of the rice. Then cover with another heaped tablespoon of rice, and mould into a ball about the size of an orange. Or, if you want to be fancy, extend the top into a pear shape. Make four balls like this.

RECIPE CONTINUES ON PAGE 97

Add a pinch of salt to the egg whites and beat them with a whisk until they start to thicken. Roll the *arancini* in the flour, dip them into the egg white mixture, then coat them thoroughly in breadcrumbs. Place on a baking tray.

Heat the remaining *ragú* sauce. Bake the *arancini* in the preheated oven for 10 minutes. Remove, put one on each plate, and pour 2 tablespoons of hot *ragú* sauce over each. Sprinkle with more parmesan.

A simpler method for smaller *arancini*: Forget the chicken livers and the quails' eggs. Make the rice mixture as above, put a smaller quantity into your palm, add two cubes of cheese and a few peas, add more rice and mould into a ball about the size of a mandarin. You should be able to make at least 12 balls. Dip them into the flour, egg whites and breadcrumbs as described above. In a small wok or deep-sided pan, fry the balls in about 6 cm (2½ inches) of vegetable oil until they are golden, about 5 minutes.

TIME 1 HOUR 30 MINUTES • SERVES 4

Here's a hearty winter filler that redeems the reputation of sadly maligned cabbage. The bacon and provolone cheese give it a great flavour. This is a typical Neapolitan dish that has nothing to do with that northern food called risotto.

9. Verzi e risi
Rice with bacon and cabbage

1 onion, finely chopped
150 g (5 oz) pancetta (or bacon)
3 tbsp olive oil
1 litre (35 fl oz) beef stock
600 g (1 lb 3½ oz) savoy cabbage, finely chopped
500 g (1 lb) arborio rice
100 g (3½ oz) provolone dolce cheese (or smoked provola), cubed
100 g (3½ oz) freshly grated parmesan cheese
salt and freshly ground black pepper

Put the onion, pancetta and oil in a large saucepan and cook uncovered over medium heat for 10 minutes. When the onion has started to caramelise, add the beef stock and bring to the boil. Add the chopped cabbage and cook for another 10 minutes. Add the rice and cook until the liquid has been absorbed, a further 15 minutes or so. Add the cubed provolone and then the parmesan, stirring after each addition. Season with salt and pepper to taste and serve.

TIME 40 MINUTES • SERVES 4

You can pretty much use any fish you like in this soup (which is really more of a stew), but rock cod is essential because it has such beautiful sweet flesh when it's cooked and an ideal texture. It's important to cook the different fish for different times because you want them to retain their flavour and texture. The only ingredients that are cooked in the oven, for example, are the calamari and octopus. Serve this with crusty bread.

10. Zuppa di pesce
Fish stew

8 clams

8 rings calamari

2 baby octopus, roughly chopped

6 mussels

125 ml (4 fl oz) olive oil

3 cloves garlic, chopped

1 rock cod, about 250 g (8 oz)

150 g (5 oz) trevalla (blue eye cod) fillets

150 g (5 oz) kingfish fillets

250 ml (8 fl oz) white wine

200 g (6½ oz) cherry tomatoes, halved

4 tbsp chopped roma tomatoes

½ blue swimmer crab

10 parsley leaves, chopped, for garnish

salt to taste

Soak the clams for 3 hours to remove any sand. Clean the calamari and octopus. Scrub the mussels and remove their beards.

Preheat the oven to 180°C (350°F/gas 4). Put the olive oil and garlic in a large ovenproof pan or casserole dish and cook until the garlic is golden, about 2 minutes. Add the calamari and octopus. Toss and cook over medium heat for 5 minutes. Add the whole rock cod and brown for 2 minutes on each side, then add the trevalla, kingfish, mussels and clams. Pour in the wine and cook on high heat until it evaporates, about 5 minutes. With a slotted spoon, remove all the seafood apart from the octopus and calamari, and set aside. Add the cherry and roma tomatoes to the pan.

Cover the pan or casserole dish and place it in the preheated oven for 15 minutes. Take the pan out of the oven and add the reserved seafood and the swimmer crab, plus a little water if it seems to be drying out. Put back in the oven for another 10 minutes. Add salt to taste.

Place the *zuppa* in a heated serving dish and serve immediately, sprinkled with parsley.

TIME 3 HOURS 40 MINUTES, INCLUDING SOAKING • SERVES 4

The Italian name for this dish means 'fish with mad water'. Presumably the inventor thought the water was mad because it had been boiling vigorously with pasta. Don't attempt this recipe if you haven't got pasta cooking water at the ready—the starchy water gives a creaminess to the tomato sauce in which the fish is cooked. I've suggested trevalla (which used to be called blue eye cod) but any meaty fish would be fine to share the madness.

11. Ricciola acqua pazza
Trevalla with cherry tomato sauce

4 cloves garlic, peeled
6 tbsp olive oil
4 x 180 g (6 oz) trevalla (blue eye cod) fillets or other firm fish
800 g (1 lb 10 oz) cherry tomatoes, halved
5 tbsp pasta cooking water
6 basil leaves, torn
salt to taste

Preheat the oven to 200°C (400°F/gas 6). Sauté the whole garlic cloves in the olive oil in an ovenproof frying pan until golden, about 2 minutes. Add the fish and cook for 1 minute on each side. Add the tomatoes.

Place the frying pan in the preheated oven for 6 minutes. Remove the fish from the pan and set aside; discard the garlic. Add the pasta cooking water. Place the pan over medium heat on the top of the stove and reduce the liquid, at the same time squashing the cherry tomatoes with a wooden spoon. Simmer for 5 minutes.

Return the fish to the pan and heat for 2 minutes. Season with salt to taste. Sprinkle with the torn basil leaves and serve immediately.
TIME 20 MINUTES • SERVES 4

Many people say they don't like tripe, but what they mean is they don't like the idea of it because it is made from one or more of the stomachs of a cow. I think most would change their minds once they'd tried this recipe, which was inspired by my experience at a restaurant called Il Desco in Verona. Their version was so sweet and tender I had to order a second plate, causing the chef to come out of the kitchen to find out who was this crazy customer. The trick is to cook the onions for a very long time and the tripe for even longer.

I suggest you ask the butcher for what is called 'green tripe' rather than bleached tripe, which has a chemical taste. As long as you wash it thoroughly, you'll get an impressive result.

This recipe makes enough for eight people, or two servings for four people, since it tastes even better a day after it is cooked.

12. Trippa alla veronese
Tripe, Verona style

500 g (1 lb) bible tripe (green if possible)
500 g (1 lb) honeycomb tripe (green if possible)
6 onions, chopped
2 tbsp olive oil
½ stick celery, chopped
3 small carrots, chopped
500 ml (16 fl oz) beef stock
100 g (3½ oz) freshly grated parmesan cheese
salt and freshly ground black pepper

Wash the tripe by leaving it under cold running water for an hour. In a large covered saucepan, boil the bible tripe with a lot of salted water for 6 hours. Then throw in the honeycomb tripe and continue boiling for another 2 hours. Drain off the water and cut the tripe into small pieces.

In a saucepan large enough to hold all the tripe, cook the onions in the olive oil over medium heat for 20 minutes. Add the celery and carrots and cook for a further 5 minutes. Add the tripe and stir to coat thoroughly, about 2 minutes. Pour in the stock and 500 ml (16 fl oz) of water, bring to the boil and simmer for 3 hours. If the tripe seems to be drying out, add a little more water but not too much—in the end you want it in a rich gravy, rather than a soup. Add salt and pepper to taste and serve with a generous sprinkling of freshly grated parmesan.

TIME 12 HOURS 30 MINUTES, INCLUDING SOAKING • SERVES 8

Quails are the nearest we can get to the highly prized game birds that are hunted all over Italy. The favourite Italian way of eating them is stuffed and roasted. This is a very pretty dish with fine colour contrasts, and the sharpness of the capsicum matches the richness of the meat. Ask your butcher for enough caul to wrap up eight quails.

13. Quaglie con peperoni
Baked quails stuffed with yellow capsicum

8 quails, deboned (ask your butcher to do it)
caul fat
200 g (6½ oz) English spinach, trimmed
8 cherry tomatoes, halved
olive oil for frying
325 ml (10½ fl oz) chicken (or game) stock

FOR THE STUFFING
2 yellow capsicums
3 tbsp finely chopped parsley
20 black olives, pitted and halved
1 clove garlic, chopped
5 tsp capers
5 tbsp dry breadcrumbs
5 tbsp extra virgin olive oil
400 g (13 oz) smoked provola cheese (or mozzarella), diced
2 anchovy fillets
salt and freshly ground black pepper

Preheat the oven to 200°C (400°F/gas 6). To make the stuffing for the quails, peel the capsicums by burning the skins directly over a gas flame or under a grill. Remove the top, the skin and seeds, and dice the flesh into small cubes about 1 cm (½ inch) square. Place the capsicums in a bowl with 2 tablespoons of the parsley, the olives, garlic, 4 teaspoons of the capers and 4 tablespoons of the breadcrumbs. Add 4 tablespoons of the extra virgin olive oil and season with salt and pepper. Mix well. Divide the stuffing into eight parts and stuff each quail. Close and wrap with caul. Secure with a toothpick at the breast.

Put a little water in a saucepan and cook the spinach leaves for 2 minutes. Drain and squeeze the leaves dry. Chop coarsely.

Slightly hollow out the centres of the cherry tomato halves. Mix the provola, anchovy fillets and the remaining parsley, capers and breadcrumbs with the remaining extra virgin olive oil and fill the tomato halves with the mixture.

Heat a little olive oil in large ovenproof frying pan. Brown the quails over high heat for 2 minutes on each side, then place in the preheated oven for 15 minutes, adding the stuffed tomatoes for the last 2 minutes. Meanwhile, heat the spinach with 125 ml (4 fl oz) of the stock. Warm the remaining stock in a separate saucepan. Remove the quails and tomatoes from the oven and cut the quails in half.

To serve, place some spinach in the middle of each plate, and top with four segments of quail and two cherry tomatoes. Pour the remaining stock over the quails.

TIME 45 MINUTES • SERVES 4

This is my variation on the classic *Tournedos Rossini*, named after the great nineteenth-century Italian composer. These are not times when we need to be importing *foie gras* and other expensive ingredients. Let's use home-grown beef, onions, potatoes and the invigorating herb, marjoram. Serve the fillet with steamed broccoli (see page 24).

14. Filetto alla marjorana
Beef with marjoram

4 x 180 g (6 oz) slices beef fillet
4 rashers bacon
2 onions, chopped
4 tbsp olive oil, plus extra for frying
leaves from 2 sprigs marjoram
125 ml (4 fl oz) dry Marsala
250 ml (8 fl oz) beef stock
3 potatoes, peeled
2 eggs
100 g (3½ oz) freshly grated
    parmesan cheese
2 tbsp finely chopped parsley
salt and freshly ground black
    pepper

Preheat the oven to 180°C (350°F/gas 4). Wrap the beef fillets with the bacon, secure with toothpicks and set aside. Caramelise the onions in the olive oil in a small saucepan over low heat for 10 minutes, then add the marjoram leaves and cook for a further 5 minutes. Pour in the Marsala and continue cooking for 10 minutes so the alcohol reduces—it doesn't matter if it flames. Add the beef stock and let it reduce for 5 more minutes. Set aside.

Cook the potatoes in boiling water, drain and mash. Let them cool down, then add the eggs, parmesan, parsley, salt and pepper; stir well. Shape the potato mixture into four flat pancakes, each about 2 cm (¾ inch) thick and the size of a beef fillet. Put a little olive oil in a frying pan, bring the heat to high, and fry the pancakes for about 6 minutes on each side until they are crunchy. Put the pancakes on four serving plates and keep warm.

Meanwhile, cook the beef. Put a little oil on a hot plate or frying pan. Sear the fillets on each side for 2 minutes. Then put them in the preheated oven for 8 minutes. Remove the meat and turn off the oven. Let the fillets rest for 10 minutes, then return them to the oven for a couple of minutes to warm before serving. Heat the sauce gently.

To serve, place the fillets on top of the pancakes and pour a generous amount of sauce over them.

TIME 1 HOUR • SERVES 4

In Naples we call these rolls *braciolette*. In other parts of Italy they're called *involtini*. Whatever name you use, please take my advice: the point here is to serve the rolls with a lush ripe tomato sauce, so if possible leave the tomatoes out in the sun for 24 hours before you cook the dish. Roast potatoes are a fine accompaniment.

15. Braciolette napoletana
Rolled veal with pine nuts and raisins

8 thin slices veal, each about
    80 g (2½ oz)
1 onion, chopped
6 tbsp olive oil, plus extra for frying
375 ml (12 fl oz) red wine
400 g (13 oz) tomatoes, chopped
1 tbsp finely chopped parsley

FOR THE FILLING
40 g (1½ oz) pine nuts
40 g (1½ oz) raisins
2 tbsp freshly grated parmesan
    cheese
4 tbsp finely chopped parsley
2 cloves garlic, finely chopped
2 tbsp olive oil
salt and freshly ground black
    pepper

FOR THE DRESSING
3 tbsp chopped parsley
2 tbsp olive oil

For the filling, in a frying pan, toss the pine nuts over medium heat with just a little olive oil until they start to turn golden. This should not take more than 2 minutes—keep moving them round and watch them closely so they don't burn. Soak the raisins in warm water for 10 minutes, then drain and squeeze out the water. Mix together the pine nuts, raisins, parmesan, parsley, garlic, olive oil, salt and pepper.

Lay out the slices of veal on a board, cover them with plastic wrap and pound with a mallet until thin. Place about 1 tablespoon of the filling along the length of each slice, leaving about 1 cm (½ inch) of meat on either side of the mixture. Roll each piece of veal into a cylinder and secure the ends with toothpicks.

In a frying pan, cook the onion in the olive oil over medium heat until golden, about 8 minutes. Lower the heat, add the veal rolls and brown, turning them often, about 4 minutes. Add the red wine, raise the heat to medium and allow the wine to reduce for about 5 minutes. Add the tomatoes and continue cooking over medium heat for 20 minutes.

Place the veal rolls on a serving dish and remove the toothpicks. Pour over the tomato sauce, sprinkle on the parsley. If you want to serve this with a dressing, puree the parsley and olive oil in a blender and drizzle a little on each plate.

TIME 1 HOUR • SERVES 4

This is named after my most loyal customer for 30 years, the Sydney jeweller Reg Wickers. He fell in love with this variant of *involtini* one day, and spread the word to other customers, who now come in and ask for 'Reg's favourite'. Serve it with baked potatoes.

16. Braciolette Reginaldo
Veal rolls, Reg style

400 g (13 oz) English spinach,
    trimmed and chopped
70 g (2½ oz) butter
100 g (3½ oz) freshly grated
    parmesan cheese
sprinkle of nutmeg
8 thin slices veal
200 g (6½ oz) dry breadcrumbs
olive oil for frying
juice of ½ lemon
4 tbsp extra virgin olive oil
1 tbsp finely chopped parsley
salt and freshly ground black
    pepper

Put a little water in a saucepan and cook the spinach leaves for 2 minutes. Drain and squeeze the leaves dry. Put them in a frying pan with the butter, parmesan and nutmeg and toss them over medium heat for 5 minutes.

Let the mixture cool, then place a spoonful lengthways across the middle of each veal slice, leaving about 1 cm (½ inch) of meat on each side. Roll each slice up into a cylinder, secure with toothpicks and then roll them in the breadcrumbs.

Preheat a heavy-based frying pan, pour in some olive oil and put in the veal rolls. Brown them, using tongs to turn them often, and splash on more olive oil when needed. The aim is to create a crunchy exterior, which should take about 6 minutes.

To make the sauce, mix the lemon juice with the extra virgin olive oil, whisking vigorously until it becomes thicker and frothy. Season to taste.

Place two rolls on each serving plate, remove the toothpicks, pour over the sauce, sprinkle over the parsley and serve immediately.
TIME 25 MINUTES • SERVES 4

The classic Milanese dish translates literally as 'bone hole' because the most important part is the marrow in the middle of the shank. Many modern recipes include tomatoes, but I've used a little Marsala instead.

Ask your butcher for beef *ossobuco* rather than veal *ossobuco* because the beef has more flavour. And don't forget to give your guests teaspoons so they can scoop out the marrow. Serve with mashed potato.

17. Ossobuco alla genovese
Beef shanks with Marsala

10 medium onions, chopped
125 ml (4 fl oz) olive oil
3 small carrots, chopped
1 stick celery, chopped
8 pieces beef shin, each about
   350 g (11½ oz)
flour for dusting
1 litre (35 fl oz) dry white wine
125 ml (4 fl oz) dry Marsala
leaves from 5 sprigs marjoram
salt and freshly ground black
   pepper

Preheat the oven to 200°C (400°F/gas 6). In a large heavy-based casserole dish, sauté the onions in the olive oil over medium heat for 5 minutes, then add the carrots and celery and cook for another 5 minutes. Dust the pieces of *ossobuco* in flour, add them to the casserole, turn the heat up to high and brown the pieces on all sides, for about 10 minutes total time. Add the white wine and enough water to cover the meat. Cover the casserole and cook in the hot oven for 90 minutes. Take the casserole out and put it on the stove over low heat. Add the Marsala and simmer for 10 minutes. Add the marjoram, stir and simmer for another 2 minutes. Turn off the heat.

Serve two pieces of *ossobuco* per plate, ideally with mashed potato.

TIME 2 HOURS • SERVES 4

This dish is named after my farm, Valleyfield, north of Sydney. There are plenty of wild rabbits there but they're too tough to eat. For this dish I would always use farmed white rabbits—get the butcher to cut up the rabbit. Serve it with wet polenta.

18. Coniglio alla Valleyfield
Rabbit, home style

1 onion, chopped
2 carrots, chopped
185 ml (6 fl oz) olive oil
1 mild red chilli to taste, cut in
    half and seeds removed
1 rabbit, cut into 7 pieces
500 ml (16 fl oz) white wine
5 roma tomatoes, chopped
leaves of 2 stems rosemary, finely
    chopped
leaves of 4 sprigs thyme, chopped
salt

Sauté the onion and carrot in a casserole dish with the olive oil over medium heat until the onion is golden, about 8 minutes. Add the chilli and cook for another 2 minutes.

Add the rabbit pieces and brown for 5 minutes. Pour in the wine and cook until almost evaporated, about 5 minutes. Then add the tomatoes, rosemary and thyme. Pour over 250 ml (8 fl oz) of water. Cook slowly, uncovered, for about 1 hour. Check several times while cooking—if it seems to be drying out, add more water. Season with salt to taste.

TIME 1 HOUR 20 MINUTES • SERVES 4

Rhubarb seems to have originated in China and was discussed at length by Marco Polo in his account of travels from Venice in the thirteenth century. Italians apparently regarded it as medicine until the 1800s, when pie recipes a little bit like this began to appear. Serve the tart with vanilla ice-cream.

19. Torta di rabarbaro
Rhubarb tart

FOR THE PASTRY
250 g (8 oz) flour
100 g (3½ oz) caster sugar
150 g (5 oz) unsalted butter,
    at room temperature
1 egg

FOR THE FILLING
600 g (1 lb 3½ oz) rhubarb,
    trimmed and cubed
230 g (7½ oz) sugar
½ tbsp unsalted butter
1 granny smith apple, peeled, cored
    and cubed
1 tsp ground cinnamon
2 tsp unsalted pistachio nuts,
    shelled
zest of ½ orange
1 egg, beaten
icing sugar for dusting

4 x 10-cm (4-inch) diameter
    crinkly edged tart tins

Place the flour in a bowl and add the caster sugar, softened butter and egg. Mix well. Knead it gently and shape into a ball. Roll the dough in plastic wrap and chill in the fridge for 1 hour. Preheat the oven to 180°C (350°F/gas 4).

Remove the pastry from the fridge and leave to sit for 5 minutes at room temperature. Roll it out on a floured benchtop to 5 mm (¼ inch) thickness, cut four circles about 11 cm (4½ inches) in diameter and line the base and sides of the buttered tart tins. Gather the remaining dough into a ball; set it aside in the fridge for decorating the tarts later.

Prick the base of each pastry case with a fork. To blind bake the pastry, line each tart with greaseproof paper or foil and weigh it down with dried beans or uncooked rice. Bake in the preheated oven until golden, about 15 minutes. Remove from the oven, remove the beans and allow to cool.

Place the rhubarb in a saucepan with 200 g (6½ oz) of the sugar and simmer until soft, about 10 minutes, then allow to cool. Melt the unsalted butter in a frying pan. Add the apple cubes and stir to coat with the remaining 30 g (1 oz) of sugar and the cinnamon. Cook over low heat for 8 minutes, then allow to cool. Dry-roast the pistachio nuts in a hot frying pan, tossing them over high heat for 2 minutes, watching to make sure they don't burn.

In a bowl, mix together the apple, rhubarb, pistachio nuts and orange zest. Fill the pastry shells with this fruit mixture. Cut the remaining pastry into 1-cm (½-inch) strips and use to decorate the tops of the tarts in a lattice pattern. Brush the beaten egg over the pastry strips. Place the tarts in the oven and bake until the tops are golden, about 5 minutes. Remove the tarts from the tins, dust with icing sugar and serve.

TIME 1 HOUR 45 MINUTES • SERVES 4

There are people who are bemused by the idea of eating eggplant as a dessert—particularly eggplant combined with chocolate—but it's a Naples tradition going back at least a hundred years. In my restaurant I like to challenge conservative tastes by decorating it with edible gold leaf (which you can buy from art shops quite cheaply). But you may be relieved to know the gold is not essential for the taste.

20. Involtini di melanzane con ricotta e cioccolato

Chocolate eggplant

2 large eggplants
flour for dusting
olive oil for frying
2 eggs
50 g (1¾ oz) icing sugar, sieved
½ tsp ground cinnamon
4 squares of gold leaf for
   decoration (optional)

FOR THE FILLING
400 g (13 oz) ricotta cheese, sieved
100 g (3½ oz) icing sugar, sieved
100 g (3½ oz) candied fruit, diced
   small, plus extra for serving
50 ml (1¾ fl oz) orange blossom
   water.

FOR THE CHOCOLATE SAUCE
250 ml (8 fl oz) cream
250 g (8 oz) chocolate, 70 per cent
   cocoa

Peel the eggplants and slice each lengthways into four pieces, each about 1 cm (½ inch) thick. Lightly dust them with flour. Pour 6 cm (2½ inches) of olive oil into a wok or deep frying pan and heat until it sizzles when a drop of water is thrown in, then fry the eggplant slices until golden, about 1 minute each side. Drain them on paper towels and let them cool.

In a bowl, beat the eggs, icing sugar and cinnamon together. Dip the eggplants in the egg mixture. Add more oil to the wok, turn up the heat and fry the eggplants again, about 30 seconds each side. Drain on paper towels.

For the filling, place all the ingredients in a bowl and beat together with a wooden spoon. Lay each piece of eggplant on a board, spread 1 tablespoon of the ricotta filling lengthways along each piece, and roll each into a log.

For the sauce, bring the cream to the boil in a small saucepan, reduce the heat, add the chocolate and stir until it has melted.

To serve, place two eggplant rolls on each plate and pour over the chocolate sauce. Scatter some candied fruit around each plate and put a little gold leaf on the top.

TIME 45 MINUTES • SERVES 4

We eat this pie in Naples at Easter time. Apparently its origins date from the ancient Roman habit of celebrating the fertility of spring by eating whole grains of spelt wheat (*farro*). We use whole wheat kernels, available from health food shops, and soak them overnight. You can buy wheat grains that have been soaked (*gran cotto*). The pie contains a little pork fat, which is essential to the texture and flavour. The wholesomeness of everything else makes up for it.

21. Pastiera
Wheat and ricotta pie

FOR THE FILLING

300 g (10 oz) whole wheat kernels
  (or *gran cotto*)
1 tbsp pork dripping
pinch of salt
1 litre (35 fl oz) milk
10 g (⅔ oz) ground cinnamon
½ vanilla stick
zest of 1 lemon, very finely sliced
500 g (1 lb) ricotta cheese
zest of 1 orange, very finely sliced
250 g (8 oz) candied fruit
125 ml (4 fl oz) orange blossom
  water
100 ml (3½ fl oz) Strega liqueur
6 eggs, separated
6 tbsp sugar
icing sugar for dusting

FOR THE PASTRY

500 g (1 lb) flour
200 g (6½ oz) sugar
pinch of salt
300 g (10 oz) butter, cut into
  small cubes
1 egg

1 x tart tin, 26 cm diameter
  x 5 cm deep (10 x 2 inches)

Put the whole wheat into a large saucepan, cover with 2 litres (72 fl oz) of cold water and add the pork dripping and a pinch of salt. Bring to the boil and simmer, covered, for 3 hours. Strain and put it back into the saucepan. Add the milk, cinnamon, vanilla and lemon zest. Cook for another 2 hours until the wheat resembles porridge. If it starts to dry out, add more milk. Set aside to cool. If using *gran cotto*, skip the initial 3 hours of cooking. Put the grains in the saucepan with the milk and flavourings and cook for 2 hours as described above.

For the pastry, mix together the flour, sugar and salt, then rub in the butter. Beat the egg with a fork and knead it with the flour. Gather the dough into a ball and wrap in plastic wrap. Chill in the fridge for at least 1 hour.

Preheat the oven to 180°C (350°F/gas 4). Sprinkle flour on a benchtop and on a rolling pin, and roll out the dough to about 5 mm (¼ inch) thickness. Cut out a large circle of pastry wide enough to line the base and sides of the buttered tart tin. Cut off the excess pastry, gather it into a ball and set it aside in the fridge for decorating the pie later.

Sieve the ricotta into a large bowl. Add the 'porridge', orange zest, candied fruit, orange flower water and Strega. Mix well. Beat the egg yolks and the sugar until smooth and creamy, then add to the ricotta mixture. Beat the egg whites with a pinch of salt until stiff with a whisk or an egg beater and gently fold into the ricotta mixture.

Pour the filling into the pastry case. Cut the remaining pastry into strips about 1 cm (½ inch) wide and lay the strips across the pie in a lattice pattern. Where they meet at the edges, press the pastry case and lattice strips together. Bake in the preheated oven for 45 minutes. Cool.

To serve, dust with icing sugar. It is good with a scoop of vanilla ice-cream.
TIME 6 HOURS (3 HOURS IF USING PRECOOKED GRAINS) • SERVES 4

Of course I had to include a tiramisu, since it's the dessert that conquered the world. It took just 40 years to spread from Treviso, the town in north-eastern Italy where it was invented in the early 1970s, to the tiniest cafés in the most isolated villages in America, Britain, Australia and New Zealand. Its success is built upon the contrast of bitter coffee and sweet creamy mascarpone. But I decided that isn't enough. So I've added fresh figs.

22. Tiramisu con fichi
Fig and mascarpone tart

36 savoiardi (sponge-finger) biscuits
500 ml (16 fl oz) strong black coffee, cooled
6 tbsp coffee liqueur (Kahlua or Tia Maria)
750 g (1 lb 8 oz) whipped mascarpone (see recipe, page 74)
10 large fresh figs

Dip 12 of the biscuits in the coffee and lay them, side by side, along the base of a deep-sided dish. Brush them with a generous amount of liqueur and cover with whipped mascarpone.

Cut the figs into 1-cm (½-inch) thick slices and put a layer of them over the mascarpone. Make another layer of biscuits (dipped in the coffee and brushed with the liqueur), mascarpone and figs. If there's space, make a third layer, finishing with all the remaining mascarpone. Cover the dish with plastic wrap and refrigerate for 3 hours before serving.

TIME 3 HOURS 30 MINUTES, INCLUDING CHILLING • SERVES 4

Serve this nougat semifreddo with spoonfuls of ripe persimmons (if they're in season) or some fresh raspberries or sliced strawberries and fresh mint leaves.

23. Semifreddo al torrone
Nougat semifreddo

600 ml (19 fl oz) cream
50 ml (1¾ fl oz) Strega
50 ml (1¾ fl oz) Marsala
6 eggs, separated, from which you use 6 yolks and 3 whites
4 tbsp caster sugar
250 g (8 oz) hard nougat, finely crushed

In a large bowl, whisk the cream until stiff, then whisk the Strega and Marsala through the cream. In a separate bowl, whisk the 6 egg yolks and sugar together until light and fluffy. Using a spatula, fold the yolks into the cream mixture. In a clean bowl, whisk the 3 egg whites until they form stiff peaks. Gently fold them into the cream mixture. Gradually and gently fold in the nougat. Freeze for at least 4 hours.

Cut into slices and serve each with persimmons or berries and a mint leaf.

TIME 4 HOURS 15 MINUTES, INCLUDING CHILLING • SERVES 4

Zuccotto means 'little pumpkin'. That's a reference to the shape of this pudding, which supposedly is modelled on the dome on top of the cathedral in Florence. Put your dome in the middle of the table and let your family and guests worship by slicing generous segments for themselves. You could make four individual domes in smaller moulds: just divide the ingredients by four for each one.

24. Zuccotto
Chocolate and ricotta dome cake

125 g (4¼ oz) butter
185 g (6 oz) caster sugar
3 eggs
375 g (12 oz) flour
1½ tsp baking powder
pinch of salt
60 ml (2 fl oz) milk
1 tbsp lemon juice

FOR THE SYRUP
juice of 1 lemon
juice of 1 orange
4 tbsp sugar
100 ml (3½ fl oz) limoncello

FOR THE FILLING
100 g (3½ oz) slivered almonds
100 g (3½ oz) hazelnuts
250 ml (8 fl oz) cream
100 g (3½ oz) icing sugar
160 g (5½ oz) mascarpone
100 g (3½ oz) ricotta cheese
200 g (6½ oz) candied fruit
300 g (10 oz) dark chocolate, finely
   chopped

1 x 20-cm (7½-inch) diameter
   springform cake tin
1 x 26-cm (10-inch) diameter
   stainless steel pudding bowl,
   about 10 cm (4 inches) deep

First make the cake. Preheat the oven to 180°C (350°F/gas 4) and line the cake tin with buttered greaseproof paper. Beat the butter and sugar together until light and fluffy. Add the eggs gradually, and then gently fold in the flour, baking powder and salt. Add the milk and the lemon juice gently; mix well. Pour the mixture into the lined cake tin and bake until golden and firm, about 30 minutes. Turn the cake out and cool on a rack.

To make the syrup, in a small saucepan combine the lemon and orange juices, 100 ml (3½ fl oz) of water and the sugar. Boil for 1 minute. Cool and add the limoncello. Set aside.

For the filling, dry-roast the almonds and hazelnuts in a frying pan over medium heat for 4 minutes, then chop the hazelnuts. Whisk the cream and icing sugar together until stiff. Fold in the mascarpone and ricotta and keep whisking until smooth. Gently fold in the nuts.

Line the pudding bowl with plastic wrap so the film comes over the top and overlaps the sides. Slice the cake into triangles 5 mm (¼ inch) thick and long enough to cover two-thirds the height of the bowl. Line the base of the bowl with the triangles, tips at the centre; the bottom should be completely covered. Brush the triangles of cake with syrup so it is completely soaked.

Divide the ricotta filling into two equal portions. Mix the candied fruit into one portion and fill the cake-lined part of the bowl with this mixture. Melt 200 g (6½ oz) of the chocolate, cool a little, then pour into the other portion of filling and stir it through; chop the rest of the chocolate and add. Fill the remaining space in the bowl with the chocolate mixture and level out the top. Cover with the remaining cake slices. Put the bowl in the fridge for 2 hours.

To serve, pull inwards on the plastic wrap to loosen the *zucotto*, then turn the moulded cake out onto a big platter. Remove the plastic wrap and serve the *zucotto* as slices, with whipped cream.

TIME 3 HOURS 30 MINUTES, INCLUDING CHILLING • SERVES 4

4

spectacular
sensations

Well, there's restaurant food and there's domestic food, and never the twain shall meet. Except here, in this book. I agree with the theory that people eat out in order to enjoy experiences they'd never have at home. Restaurant kitchens possess the staff, the equipment and the training to indulge a chef's most lavish fantasies. At home that's going to be too much trouble. Or is it?

There are times when you're enjoying an ingenious creation in a great restaurant—hopefully mine—and one of your foodie friends says, 'This is amazing. You'd be crazy to try this at home.' But you think, 'Yep, I'm that crazy.' It's great to be ambitious. And if you're prepared to put in the time and effort, I'm happy to help with ideas and tips that should let you amaze your guests.

Some of the recipes will turn out better if you have special equipment, but if you don't I've suggested alternatives that will let you come close. Some of the ingredients may not be in your local supermarket, but it will be fun to go hunting in greengrocers and specialist delis. Some are highly seasonal, which makes them rare treats. Some ingredients—such as cream, cheese and pork dripping—may be on the banned lists of fitness fanatics, but you're not going to be eating these dishes every day. These recipes are for moments of celebration, when hospitality and self-indulgence overflow.

Although this is special occasion food, there will be plenty of opportunities to involve kids (of all ages) in the making of these recipes. In my restaurant I have a whole kitchen brigade who can indulge my whims whenever I need ingredients finely chopped or whipped or stuffed or seared or watched over. If you've followed my suggestions in chapter 2, you should by now have your own brigade of enthusiasts to help in your kitchen and to beam with pride when their contribution is acclaimed by your guests. Just be sure an adult is present whenever heat or sharp knives or strong shoulders are required.

That's not to suggest these recipes are difficult and dangerous. Most of them require only that you spend time and care in preparation. Many are quick and simple, even if the ingredients are exotic. After all, this is Italian cooking—how hard can it be?

1. **Pure di cannellini con cappesante** Scallops with cannellini bean puree and crispy pancetta

2. **Leatherjacket 'Usuzukuri'** Marinated raw leatherjacket

3. **Fichi biondi** Baked figs with gorgonzola sauce

4. **Zuppa di diavoletti** Tomato and prawn soup

5. **Tortino di patate** Potato, olive and anchovy tortino

6. **Risotto con zucca** Pumpkin risotto in pumpkins

7. **Risotto con pere e taleggio** Pear and cheese risotto

8. **Rigatoni con salsa di scorfano** Pasta with rock cod sauce

9. **Ravioli reali** Ravioli with spinach and egg yolks

10. **Pappardelle alla lepre** Pasta with hare sauce

11. **Timballo** The pasta stockade

12. **San Pietro con erbe acetosa** John Dory with sorrel sauce

13. **San Pietro con carciofi** John Dory with globe artichokes

14. **Pesce al Barolo** Roasted blue eye with pancetta and red wine sauce

15. **Porchetta** Stuffed pork

16. **Capretto con piselli** Casserole of baby goat with peas

17. **Galletto ripieni con ortiche** Spatchcock with nettle stuffing

18. **Cervo alla valtellina** Medallions of venison with pureed beetroot and pumpkin gnocchi

19. **Cioccolato verona** Chocolate layer cake

20. **Mille mele** Baked apple cake

21. **Millefoglie** Puff pastry with strawberries and hazelnuts

22. **Chiacchiere** Cinnamon pastries

This is one of those flavour combinations made in heaven—scallops and rosemary, delivered to the palate by a creamy bean puree. It looks so pretty, it demands to be served on fine china.

1. Pure di cannellini con cappesante
Scallops with cannellini bean puree and crispy pancetta

300 g (10 oz) cannellini beans
leaves of 3 stems rosemary, finely
　　chopped
60 ml (2 fl oz) extra virgin olive oil,
　　plus extra for serving
16 scallops, roe off
16 thin slices prosciutto
1 tsp olive oil
freshly ground pepper

Place the beans in a large saucepan, cover with water and soak them for at least 6 hours. Drain and replace the water. Bring to the boil and simmer until the beans are tender, about 1 hour. Drain the beans, reserving some of the cooking water.

Preheat the oven to 180°C (350°F/gas 4). Place the beans in a blender with the rosemary, extra virgin olive oil and two grinds of pepper. Puree. If the paste seems dry and thick, add a little water from the beans.

Wrap each of the scallops in one slice of prosciutto, which should go round the scallop about three times (it is not necessary to use a toothpick to secure it). Put the olive oil in an ovenproof frying pan over high heat. Once the oil is hot, add the scallops and sear for 1 minute on each side. Then put the pan in the preheated oven and roast for 5 minutes.

Pour a generous dollop of the bean puree onto each plate. Sit four scallops on each and drizzle with thin lines of extra virgin olive oil.

TIME 7 HOURS 15 MINUTES, INCLUDING SOAKING • SERVES 4

Let me introduce a special guest star—my friend Tetsuya Wakuda, who runs a pretty successful restaurant in Sydney. He often drops by my place for a chat and we've been amazed at how closely his Japanese approach to ingredients fits with my Italian approach. He kindly contributed this recipe for a delicate 'carpaccio' of leatherjacket, a surprisingly cheap fish which he says has a taste and a texture very like Japan's famous—and dangerous—fugu or pufferfish. Make sure you use sashimi-grade fish.

2. Leatherjacket 'Usuzukuri'
Marinated raw leatherjacket

200 g (6½ oz) leatherjacket fillets
2 tbsp extra virgin olive oil
2 tsp very finely chopped chives
freshly ground black pepper

FOR THE DRESSING
2 tbsp light soy sauce
2 tsp mirin
½ tsp freshly grated ginger
1 tsp lemon juice
pinch of caster sugar
pinch of ground white pepper

FOR THE GARNISH
20 tiny salad and herb leaves
    (mesclun, thyme, oregano)
3 or 4 stalks chives, cut into pieces
    about 1 cm (½ inch) long
1 cm (½ inch) white part of 1 leek,
    julienned
sea salt flakes

Using a sharp, flat-bladed knife and holding it as close to horizontal as you can, slice the leatherjacket fillets into very thin layers—as thin as you can manage. Arrange the leatherjacket slices over four serving plates.

Whisk together all the dressing ingredients. Just before serving, drizzle the dressing over the slices of leatherjacket. Then drizzle with the extra virgin olive oil and season with the black pepper and finely chopped chives. Decorate with the salad leaves, chive sticks, leek slices and a little sea salt.

TIME 15 MINUTES • SERVES 4

The Italian name *fichi biondi* translates as 'blonde figs', although 'pink and blonde' would be more accurate. Actually, this is a sophisticated treat that challenges the stereotype of the dumb blonde. The most important thing is to choose the best possible figs, and that's likely to be in late summer or early autumn.

3. Fichi biondi
Baked figs with gorgonzola sauce

12 thin slices prosciutto
12 fresh figs
1 tbsp butter
425 ml (14 fl oz) cream
220 g (7½ oz) gorgonzola cheese

Preheat the oven to 200°C (400°F/gas 6). Wrap a slice of prosciutto around the middle of each fig and secure with a toothpick. Melt the butter, cream and gorgonzola together in a saucepan over low heat.

Place the figs in an ovenproof dish, pour the cream sauce over and cover the dish with foil. Bake in the preheated oven for 7 minutes. Remove the foil and bake for a further 1 minute.

To serve, arrange three figs on each serving plate and pour over the sauce. If you like, you could sprinkle a few specks of chopped parsley onto the sauce for colour.

TIME 15 MINUTES • SERVES 4

If you don't like chilli, don't bother with this. Its Italian name, 'soup of the little devils', comes from its bite. It is thick and strong and fragrant and looks wonderful served in white bowls with garlic croutons on top. If you want to give it even more guts—in winter, say—you can substitute a little pork dripping for some of the olive oil.

4. Zuppa di diavoletti
Tomato and prawn soup

2 cloves garlic, peeled and halved

2 tbsp extra virgin olive oil (or
    1 tbsp extra virgin olive oil and
    1 tbsp pork dripping)

2 small red chillies, seeded and
    finely chopped

leaves of 3 stems rosemary, finely
    chopped

3 bay leaves

400 ml (13 oz) fresh or tinned
    tomatoes, pureed

200 g (6½ oz) green school prawns,
    peeled

4 pieces bread, cut into crostini

1 tbsp olive oil

leaves of 4 sprigs parsley, coarsely
    chopped

salt to taste

Preheat the oven to 180°C (350°F/gas 4). Put 1 garlic clove into a frying pan with the extra virgin olive oil (or the olive oil and pork dripping) and sauté over medium heat until the garlic is golden, about 2 minutes. Add the chopped chillies, rosemary and bay leaves. Stirring with a wooden spoon, sauté over medium heat for 2 minutes. Pour in the tomato puree and cook for 20 minutes over low heat. Add a little water if the soup seems to be drying out.

When the tomato is cooked, remove and discard the garlic. Add the prawns. Cook for another 2 minutes. Taste for salt.

Meanwhile, make the crostini. Rub the bread with the remaining garlic halves, and then brush with the olive oil. Bake in the preheated oven for 10 minutes, then cut each piece of toast into about six pieces.

Serve in four soup plates with the crostini on top and sprinkled with the chopped parsley.

TIME 35 MINUTES • SERVES 4

The sauce for this dish goes back to the Romans, who loved to combine citrus juice and anchovies. But the Romans didn't have potatoes, which only reached Italy in the eighteenth century. Their fluffiness seems a perfect match for the sharpness of the orange and anchovy, and the toasted sesame seeds give texture and contrast. I suggest you use white anchovies, which have a more subtle flavour than the brown ones.

To present this in its most attractive way—as individual cylinders for each guest—you will need metal moulds about 6 cm (2½ inches) across. If you don't have these, you could make the tortino in a small casserole dish, layering it like a lasagne and cutting it into four slices to serve.

5. Tortino di patate
Potato, olive and anchovy tortino

300 ml (10 fl oz) extra virgin
  olive oil
100 ml (3½ fl oz) white balsamic
  vinegar (or white wine vinegar)
4 large potatoes
100 g (3½ oz) sesame seeds
160 g (5½ oz) black olives, pitted
  and roughly chopped
20 white anchovies
1 tbsp fennel seeds
4 inner leaves of curly endive,
  finely sliced
20 orange segments
250 ml (8 fl oz) orange juice

4 x metal cylinders or ramekins,
  about 6 cm diameter (2½
  inches)

For the marinade, mix together the extra virgin olive oil and vinegar. Peel the potatoes and slice finely so they are about 2.5 mm (⅛ inch) thick. With the metal mould, press down on each potato slice to cut out discs that fit the mould. Steam the potato discs for about 5 minutes. While they are still warm, put them in a bowl and pour over the oil and vinegar mixture. Let them marinate for at least 8 hours in the fridge.

Dry-roast the sesame seeds: preheat a heavy-based frying pan and toss the seeds over high heat for 2 minutes, watching to make sure they don't burn. Place a mould on a plate, and slide in one slice of potato so it rests at the bottom. Sprinkle with olives and the roasted sesame seeds. Add one anchovy, then top with another slice of potato. Repeat the process so you have six layers, varying the position of the anchovies on each layer. Fill the other three moulds in the same way, reserving a few tablespoons of the olives for the garnish, and set in the fridge for 1 hour.

Dry-roast the fennel seeds using the same method as for the sesame seeds. When you are ready to serve, push down on the potato stack with a spoon and slide the mould up and away. Scatter the slices of endive around the cylinders of potato. Arrange orange segments around the endive. Drizzle orange juice over the potatoes and endive. Sprinkle on the fennel seeds and the reserved olives and serve.

TIME 9 HOURS 15 MINUTES, INCLUDING MARINATING • SERVES 4

The impact of this dish is as much in the presentation as in the flavour—your guests have their own personal pumpkins and get to lift the lids and smell the sage and parmesan wafting up from the bright orange rice. Then they dip in and find that the pumpkin has dissolved into the rice. It is a whole new experience in risotto.

6. Risotto con zucca

Pumpkin risotto in pumpkins

4 small pumpkins, each about
   1 kg (2 lb)
2 litres (72 fl oz) chicken stock
2 tbsp chopped onion
2 tbsp unsalted butter
250 g (8 oz) arborio rice
12 sage leaves, roughly chopped
100 g (3½ oz) freshly grated
   parmesan cheese

Cut around the top of each pumpkin to make a lid. Remove the top and set aside. Scoop out the flesh inside the pumpkin and put it in a bowl. In a large saucepan, boil the four pumpkin shells for 5 minutes, take them out and leave upended so they dry out.

Bring the chicken stock to a boil in a small saucepan and keep warm over low heat as you cook the risotto. In a large frying pan, sauté the onion in the butter over medium heat until golden, about 5 minutes. Add the rice and stir for 3 minutes so the rice is thoroughly coated in the butter. Pour one ladle of warm stock into the rice and stir over medium heat until the liquid is absorbed. Add all the pumpkin flesh and one more ladle of chicken stock. Keep stirring and adding stock for 20 minutes. The pumpkin should melt into the rice. In the last 5 minutes, stir in the sage and grated parmesan.

Place each pumpkin shell on a serving plate and fill it with risotto, replace the lid and serve immediately.

TIME 45 MINUTES • SERVES 4

It's a time-consuming business, making risotto. You can't just put rice and stock together and let it boil. You must keep watching and stirring, adding a ladle of stock every few minutes and waiting for it to be absorbed into the rice. I find this a very calming activity. And after 20 minutes or so, you have to keep tasting so you can be ready to stop before it becomes too soft. Italians like their risotto *al dente*—creamy but with a little teeth-resistance in the middle. With all your tasting, try to leave a bit for your guests.

Taleggio is a melting cheese with a fruity tang that perfectly complements pears. If you can't find taleggio, you could experiment with other mild, slightly sweet cheeses, such as bel paese. The best pears for this recipe are corella or packham.

7. Risotto con pere e taleggio
Pear and cheese risotto

2 firm pears
1 litre (35 fl oz) chicken stock
1 small onion, finely sliced
1 tbsp unsalted butter
250 g (8 oz) arborio rice
150 g (5 oz) taleggio cheese, diced

Peel and dice the pears and leave in cold water so they don't go brown. Bring the chicken stock to a boil in a small saucepan and keep warm over low heat as you cook the risotto. In a large frying pan, sauté the onion in the butter over medium heat until golden, about 5 minutes. Add the rice and stir for 3 minutes until the rice is thoroughly coated with the butter.

Add one ladle of warm stock—the rice should hiss as it goes in—and keep stirring over medium heat until the liquid is absorbed. Continue this process of adding stock and stirring for about 20 minutes until the rice has expanded but remains *al dente*. Add the cheese and half the diced pears and keep stirring for just enough time to let the cheese melt through.

Divide the risotto among four bowls and sprinkle with the remaining pears. Serve immediately.

TIME 40 MINUTES • SERVES 4

Rock cod is a strong, deep-swimming fish that stands up to a lot of cooking, so it's ideal for a pasta sauce. The name of this dish is slightly misleading because the sauce also contains leatherjacket (which requires a different cooking time). And while the pasta I've named here is rigatoni, you could use any tube shape such as *mezzani* or *paccheri*.

8. Rigatoni con salsa di scorfano
Pasta with rock cod sauce

4 rock cod, each about 300 g
   (10 oz)
2 small leatherjackets, skinned
2 cloves garlic, halved
about 125 ml (4 fl oz) olive oil
150 ml (5 fl oz) dry white wine
12 ripe tomatoes, chopped
300 g (10 oz) large rigatoni (or
   other tube pasta)
2 tbsp chopped parsley
salt and freshly ground black
   pepper

Preheat the oven to 150°C (300°F/gas 2). Remove the heads and tails of all the fish. In a large casserole dish, sauté the garlic in a little olive oil until golden, about 1 minute. Add the leatherjackets. Seal both sides over medium heat, about 2 minutes on each side, adding more olive oil if necessary. Remove and set aside. Cut each rock cod in half and place in the pan. Cook over medium heat until the skin starts to break up, about 5 minutes on each side.

Remove the garlic from the pan and discard. Add the wine and bring to the boil. Simmer, uncovered, until the wine is reduced by half, about 5 minutes. Add the chopped tomatoes and bring back to the boil. Then return the leatherjackets to the pan and simmer gently until the flesh starts to fall off the bone, about 20 minutes. Remove the leatherjackets—meat and bones—from the pan and set aside. Cover the pan with a lid and cook in the preheated oven for a further 20 minutes.

Meanwhile, pick all the flesh off the bones of the leatherjackets and discard the bones. Set aside the leatherjacket flesh. Put on a saucepan of water to boil for the pasta.

Remove the pan from the oven. Pick out and discard the bones of the rock cod. Puree the rock cod and tomato mixture in a mouli or blender. Return the puree to the pan and place it over medium heat on top of the stove. Simmer and reduce the sauce for 10 minutes. At the same time, put on the pasta and cook until *al dente*, about 10 minutes.

Add the leatherjacket flesh and the strained pasta to the sauce, stirring it through. Sprinkle on the chopped parsley, season to taste and serve.

TIME 1 HOUR 30 MINUTES • SERVES 4

The Italian name of this dish translates as 'royal ravioli'—it is based on a speciality of the chef who worked for the last king of Italy (who was thrown out when the population voted to introduce a republic in 1946). The handmade ravioli are opulent verging on decadent, with a surprise package awaiting inside.

9. Ravioli reali
Ravioli with spinach and egg yolks

400 g (13 oz) flour
4 eggs
pinch of salt
basil leaves for serving

FOR THE FILLING
500 g (1 lb) English spinach,
    chopped
80 g (2½ oz) freshly grated
    parmesan cheese, plus extra
    for serving
150 g (5 oz) ricotta cheese
½ tsp nutmeg
8 egg yolks
3 amaretti biscuits, crumbled

FOR THE SAUCE
100 g (3½ oz) butter
4 tomatoes, chopped
10 basil leaves, finely chopped
salt and freshly ground black
    pepper

Make a mound of the flour on a board or benchtop and make a well in the middle. Add the eggs and a pinch of salt. Mix the flour and eggs with your hands, kneading for about 5 minutes and pushing the dough into a ball. Wrap the dough in plastic wrap and leave in the fridge for 30 minutes to relax.

Using either a rolling pin or a pasta machine, roll out the dough into thin strips. Then fold it onto itself and roll it out again. Repeat this process until the dough feels elastic, then roll the dough out into strips about 5 mm (¼ inch) thick. Cut out 16 circles from the dough, each about 10 cm (4 inches) in diameter.

To make the filling, put a little water in a saucepan and cook the spinach leaves for 5 minutes. Drain and squeeze out the water. Puree in a blender with the parmesan, ricotta and nutmeg. Spoon into a piping bag and squeeze the spinach mixture onto eight of the discs of pasta in a doughnut shape, leaving about 5 mm (¼ inch) all around the edges and a space in the middle equal to the size of an egg yolk. Place an egg yolk in each circle of spinach. Sprinkle with the crushed amaretti biscuits (about ½ teaspoon in each raviolo). Place a second pasta circle on top of the spinach and egg and press down the edges with a fork to seal the ravioli parcels. Set the ravioli aside.

For the sauce, melt the butter in a frying pan, add the chopped tomato and cook over medium to high heat for 5 minutes. Just before taking it off the heat, add the basil and salt and pepper to taste.

When you want to serve the dish, have ready a large saucepan of boiling water, add a little salt and cook the ravioli until they rise to the surface, about 3 minutes, then scoop them out with a slotted spoon and divide among four plates. Pour a little tomato sauce over each raviolo and then sprinkle on parmesan and chopped basil leaves to taste.

TIME 1 HOUR 20 MINUTES • SERVES 4

This strong-flavoured recipe is for 12 people because you're going to be buying a whole hare. The extra *ragú* can be kept in the freezer. You'll need to order the hare well in advance. Get the butcher to cut it into six pieces: two legs, two shoulders and the saddle cut in half. In midwinter, if you want to make this even more spectacular you can shave fresh black truffles over each bowl of pasta.

10. Pappardelle alla lepre
Pasta with hare sauce

1 hare, cut into 6 pieces (see above)
50 ml (1¾ oz) olive oil
6 onions, finely diced
2 carrots, finely diced
1 celery stick, finely diced
3 litres (96 fl oz) beef stock
1.5 litres (52 fl oz) milk
1 kg (2 lb) pappardelle
2 tbsp freshly grated parmesan
    cheese
leaves of 1 bunch sage, finely
    chopped
salt and freshly ground black
    pepper

FOR THE MARINADE
500 ml (16 fl oz) red wine
25 ml (1 fl oz) red wine vinegar
4 bay leaves

Place the hare pieces in a bowl, cover with all the marinade ingredients and leave in the fridge for at least 48 hours. Lift out the hare pieces and pat them dry, and put the marinade aside for later use.

On the day you are serving, preheat the oven to 180°C (350°F/gas 4). Put the olive oil in a large ovenproof casserole dish and cook the onions, carrots and celery gently without browning over low heat for 10 minutes, stirring often. Raise the heat to medium, add the pieces of hare and cook for a further 10 minutes. Pour in the marinade and bring to the boil. Add the beef stock and again bring to the boil.

Cover the casserole with a piece of baking paper then put on the lid tightly. Cook in the preheated oven until the meat is falling off the bone, about 2 hours.

Remove the hare from the casserole. Strip the meat from the bones, shred it, and put it back in the sauce. Simmer the sauce, uncovered, for another 30 minutes to reduce and thicken it. Season with salt and pepper. Add the milk and simmer for another 20 minutes. (If you plan to serve this to less than 12 people, pour some of the sauce into containers for the freezer.)

Cook the pasta in plenty of boiling salted water for about 6 minutes. Drain the pasta and add it to the sauce and cook until it's *al dente*, about another 2 minutes. Add the parmesan and chopped sage and stir through the pasta.

TIME 2 DAYS 3 HOURS, INCLUDING MARINATING ● SERVES 12

Timballo is an eighteenth-century festive dish from Naples. Originally it was a giant pie with pastry made with pork suet. Inside was a wonderful array of ingredients that enabled the host to show off his wealth. In its original form, it starred in the 1996 Stanley Tucci movie *Big Night*, in which a proud chef made a *timballo* for a food critic who never arrived.

My version is lighter but still substantial, and I'm calling it a 'stockade' in English because it seems to be surrounded by a wall of logs. I have taken away the pastry, and made it into individual servings composed in moulds (soufflé dishes are ideal) rather than a giant pie.

It's a fiddly, hands-on sort of dish, because you have to insert tiny meatballs, peas and cheese into pasta tubes—the very definition of labour-intensive. You may want to get the whole family involved. They should wash their hands thoroughly, or put on surgeon's gloves (although this makes licking your fingers less pleasant).

11. Timballo
The pasta stockade

200 g (6½ oz) shelled fresh peas
  (or frozen)
2 tbsp olive oil
1 small onion
15 quails' eggs
100 g (3½ oz) provola cheese
100 g (3½ oz) pancetta
500 g (1 lb) rigatoni, about
  60 individual pieces
120 g (4 oz) freshly grated
  parmesan cheese, plus extra
  for serving
1 egg
butter for the moulds
300 ml (10 fl oz) Napoletana sauce
  (see recipe, page 20)
chopped basil leaves for serving
salt and freshly ground black
  pepper

FOR THE TOMATO SAUCE
4 cloves garlic, peeled and flattened
125 ml (4 fl oz) olive oil
1 litre (35 fl oz) tinned tomatoes,
  crushed

For the tomato sauce, in a deep saucepan sauté the flattened garlic cloves in the olive oil over medium heat until they are golden, about 2 minutes. Add the crushed tomatoes and simmer for 5 minutes. Put in the whole basil leaves and cook for a further 15 minutes. Add salt to taste. Remove the garlic and the basil leaves. Divide the sauce between two bowls. Puree the sauce from one of the bowls using a mouli or blender.

To make the meatballs, soak the bread in the milk for 10 minutes, then squeeze out the milk. Mix the bread with the veal and egg, then stir in the parsley, salt and pepper. Knead the veal mixture and shape it into balls small enough to fit inside the rigatoni. Fry the meatballs in a little olive oil for 5 minutes until they are brown. Drain on paper towels. Add them to the bowl of tomato sauce that has not been pureed, then pour into a saucepan and simmer over low heat for 10 minutes.

Cook the fresh peas in boiling water for 8 minutes, then drain (if using frozen peas, cook for 4 minutes). In a frying pan, heat the olive oil and sauté the onion over low heat for 10 minutes; add the peas and a little salt and pepper and continue cooking for another 5 minutes.

Boil the quails' eggs for 5 minutes, peel off the shells and cut them into quarters. Set aside. Cut the provola and pancetta into cubes that are small enough to fit inside the rigatoni.

RECIPE CONTINUES ON PAGE 144

5 basil leaves
salt

FOR THE MEATBALLS
1 slice white bread, crust off
125 ml (4 fl oz) milk
200 g (6½ oz) minced veal
1 egg
1 tbsp finely chopped parsley
olive oil for frying
salt and freshly ground black
   pepper

4 x soufflé dishes, 10 cm diameter
   x 7 cm deep (4 x 2¾ inches)

Cook the rigatoni in a large saucepan of boiling water for 8 minutes—no longer or they will become too soft. Strain and put the rigatoni in a bowl of cold water to stop the cooking process. When they have cooled, put them in a tea towel to dry.

To the pureed tomato sauce, add 75 g (2½ oz) of the parmesan and the egg. Stir well and set aside 4 tablespoons for use later. Add the rigatoni to the tomato and egg mixture, and stir to coat thoroughly.

Now you're ready to build your stockade in the soufflé dishes. Rub butter all around the inside of the dishes. Cut out four circles of greaseproof paper to fit the bottom of the moulds. Cut out four rectangles of greaseproof paper about 7 cm (2¾ inches) wide and 30 cm (12 inches) long to go round the insides of the moulds. Roll each rectangle into a cylinder and stick it to the buttery walls of the soufflé dish. Stack the rigatoni in the moulds, tightly packing them. You should end up using about 13 tubes in each dish.

Into each pasta tube insert one meatball, then a little of the pea mixture, a piece each of quail's egg, provola cheese and pancetta. With your little finger or the end of a wooden spoon, pack the filling securely and add another layer of everything until you reach the top of each tube. (Any leftover meatballs and sauce can be served with spaghetti the next day.) Pour 1 tablespoon of the reserved tomato and egg mixture over each 'stockade'. Put the moulds in the refrigerator for at least 30 minutes.

Preheat the oven to 200°C (400°F/gas 6). Pour the Napoletana sauce into a saucepan and place over low heat. About 30 minutes before you're ready to serve the dish, take the rigatoni stockades out of the fridge and let them sit at room temperature for 10 minutes before putting them in the preheated oven for 15 minutes. To unmould, using oven gloves, put a serving plate on top of the mould; with one hand under the mould and one hand over the plate, flip it over so the mould is face down on the plate. Gently lift the mould up and away so the *timballo* is sitting on the plate. Remove the greaseproof paper. Pour a little Napoletana sauce over each stockade, sprinkle with the remaining parmesan and the chopped basil leaves and serve immediately.

TIME 2 HOURS • SERVES 4

Sorrel is a delicate leaf we use all too rarely in Italian cooking. If you said this dish has a certain French *haute cuisine* quality about it, I wouldn't object. There's certainly a luscious amount of cream. But the crispy calamari add Italian oomph. Serve this with a lettuce salad with a lemon vinaigrette (one part lemon juice to four parts extra virgin olive oil).

12. San Pietro con erbe acetosa

John Dory with sorrel sauce

12 black mussels, scrubbed and
    debearded
vegetable oil for frying
12 small pieces calamari
flour for dusting
4 x 150 g (5 oz) fillets John Dory
1 tbsp olive oil
salt and freshly ground black
    pepper

FOR THE SAUCE
120 ml (4 fl oz) white wine
20 ml (¾ fl oz) white wine vinegar
1 shallot, peeled and finely diced
8 black peppercorns
1 bay leaf
250 ml (8 fl oz) cream
12 sorrel leaves

Preheat the oven to 200°C (400°F/gas 6). To make the sauce, place the white wine, vinegar, shallot, peppercorns and bay leaf in an uncovered saucepan over medium heat and reduce by two-thirds, about 30 minutes. Lower the heat, add the cream and reduce for another 20 minutes.

Strain the sauce into a clean saucepan. Add the whole sorrel leaves to the sauce and heat gently for 4 minutes. Add the mussels to the cream sauce and cook until they open, about 4 minutes. Remove them from the sauce, discard the shells and set the mussel meat aside.

Heat 6 cm (2½ inches) of vegetable oil in a wok or deep frying pan to a point when a drop of water makes it sizzle. Dip each piece of calamari in the flour, shake off the excess, place in the oil and fry until golden, about 4 minutes. Scoop out, drain on paper towels and season with salt.

To cook the John Dory, add the olive oil to a non-stick frying pan and place it over medium heat. Put the fillets in the pan and sear for 1 minute each side. Then put the pan into the preheated oven for 5 minutes. Drain the cooked fish on paper towels, then season with salt and pepper.

To serve, place a piece of fish in the middle of each plate and pour the sorrel sauce all around (putting three leaves of the sorrel on each plate). Place a mussel at three points around each plate and a piece of calamari next to each mussel.

TIME 1 HOUR 15 MINUTES • SERVES 4

Artichokes are at their best in winter, and I like to make the most of them, so here I serve them in two ways—as a luscious puree and as crispy chips—and match them with a full-flavoured fish. If you can't find John Dory, you could use whiting or trevalla. But remember, the artichoke will conquer the flavour of any light white wine, so use a big woody white or forget the old matching rule and try a rosé or a pinot noir.

13. San Pietro con carciofi

John Dory with globe artichokes

7 globe artichokes
juice of ½ lemon
3 tbsp extra virgin olive oil
2 cloves garlic, crushed
flour for dusting
olive oil for frying
4 x 180 g (6 oz) John Dory fillets
1 tbsp finely chopped parsley
salt

Preheat the oven to 180°C (350°F/gas 4). Prepare five artichokes and remove the chokes (see page 88), then cut them in half. Cook them in a saucepan of boiling water with the lemon juice until tender, about 10 minutes. Drain them and dry.

Put the extra virgin olive oil and garlic in a frying pan and sauté the garlic over medium heat until golden, about 2 minutes. Add the artichoke halves and cook for another 10 minutes. Puree the artichokes, garlic and oil in a blender. Add salt to taste. Set aside.

Clean the remaining two artichokes and cut into 5-mm (¼-inch) slices. Dip them in flour and fry in 6 cm (2½ inches) of olive oil in a wok or deep frying pan over high heat until golden, about 5 minutes. Sprinkle lightly with salt.

Place the fish in a frying pan which has been coated with a little olive oil and sear for 1 minute each side. Place the pan in the preheated oven, uncovered, and bake for 4 minutes.

To serve, pour the artichoke puree down one side of each plate and arrange the John Dory in the middle. Place the fried artichokes on the other side and sprinkle the dish with parsley.

TIME 55 MINUTES • SERVES 4

We include a recipe for batter in chapter 2 and now's your chance to use it. The fried sage leaves are an ideal contrast in texture and flavour to the soft rich fish wrapped in pancetta (a kind of bacon from the stomach of the pig) and the red wine sauce made with an unusual mixture of beef and fish stocks. Instead of Barolo, you could substitute another medium-bodied red wine such as cabernet sauvignon.

14. Pesce al Barolo
Roasted blue eye with pancetta and red wine sauce

4 medium waxy potatoes
4 x 180 g (6 oz) trevalla (blue eye cod) fillets, well cleaned
20 thin slices of pancetta, about 16 x 3 cm (6 x 1¼ inches), rind removed
100 ml (3½ fl oz) olive oil
freshly ground black pepper

FOR THE SAUCE
500 ml (16 fl oz) Barolo wine
4 shallots, finely diced
1 bay leaf
60 ml (2 fl oz) beef stock
30 ml (1 fl oz) fish stock

FOR THE SAGE LEAVES
olive oil for frying
8 large sage leaves
30 ml (1 fl oz) light yeast batter (see recipe, page 44)
sea salt

Preheat the oven to 180°C (350°F/gas 4). To make the sauce, place the red wine with the shallots and bay leaf in a saucepan and simmer over low heat until the liquid is reduced by two-thirds and becomes syrupy, about 1 hour. Add the beef and fish stocks, bring to the boil and simmer for 5 minutes. Skim the sauce to remove any foam from the top and pass it through a fine sieve to remove the shallot. Set aside. Bring the sauce to a boil when you are ready to serve.

Boil the potatoes in a saucepan of water with a pinch of salt until cooked, about 15 minutes. Strain the potatoes, let them cool a little and then peel. Cut them in half.

While the potatoes are boiling, sprinkle a little pepper on each trevalla fillet and wrap with pancetta slices, using five slices per fillet. Heat the olive oil in a heavy-based ovenproof frying pan and lightly sauté each fillet for about 1 minute each side. Then place the frying pan in the preheated oven and roast the fish for about 5 minutes.

To fry the sage leaves, heat 6 cm (2½ inches) of olive oil in a wok or deep frying pan until it sizzles when a drop of water is thrown in. Dip each sage leaf in batter and fry until crisp and light golden in colour. Drain on paper towels and sprinkle on a little sea salt.

To serve, place two potato halves on each serving plate and lightly crush them with a tablespoon. Arrange the fillets on top, pour the hot sauce around the fish and place the sage leaves on top. Serve immediately with a little ground black pepper.
TIME 1 HOUR 15 MINUTES • SERVES 4

The most spectacular way to serve this *porchetta* is with a whole piglet, which you deliver to the centre of the table like a scene from a Medici banquet. Ask your butcher if he can get you a whole piglet and debone it for you. If he can't, settle for a long piece of pork loin. Also, ask the butcher for rendered pork dripping (*sugna*). Spinach is the perfect accompaniment.

15. Porchetta
Stuffed pork

1 piglet, about 3 kg (6 lb 5 oz),
   skin on and deboned (or
   2 kg/4 lb pork loin, skin on)
125 g (4¼ oz) fine salt
20 ml (¾ fl oz) olive oil

FOR THE STUFFING
2 onions, finely diced
100 g (3½ oz) unsalted butter
50 ml (1¾ oz) extra virgin olive oil
100 g (3½ oz) bacon, finely diced
250 g (8 oz) sourdough bread
50 ml (1¾ fl oz) milk
20 sage leaves, finely chopped
salt and freshly ground black
   pepper

FOR THE SUGNA SEASONING
40 g (1½ oz) rendered pork fat
   (*sugna*)
2 tsp black peppercorns, crushed
2 tsp fennel seeds, crushed
2 tsp rosemary, chopped
2 tsp sea salt
1 tsp garlic, finely chopped

Preheat the oven to maximum, at least 240°C (475°F/gas 8). To make the stuffing, stew the onions in the butter and extra virgin olive oil in a medium-sized saucepan over low heat for 1 hour, then add the bacon and cook for a further 5 minutes. Cut the sourdough bread into 2-cm (¾-inch) cubes and soak in the milk for 15 minutes. Squeeze the bread dry with your hands and add it to the onions. Add the chopped sage, mix well and remove from the heat. Season with salt and pepper to taste and set aside. To make the seasoning, melt the *sugna* and mix together with the other stuffing ingredients; set aside.

Score the skin of the piglet or pork loin: cut lengthways, then crossways, about 1 cm (½ inch) deep, so the skin is covered in 2-cm (¾-inch) squares. Turn the meat over and remove any sinew. Make a cut along its length (not right through), which enables you to flatten it out. Rub all over the fleshy surface of the meat and skin with the *sugna* seasoning, then put in the stuffing and fold the meat back over it. Fold over a large sheet of greaseproof paper and wrap it (double thickness) around the bottom and sides of the meat, leaving the top skin side open. This protects the meat while it cooks and prevents the stuffing from falling out. Secure with string: tie it tightly several times around the meat and once lengthways.

Place the meat on a stainless-steel rack in a large baking dish. Rub the skin with more *sugna* and then the fine salt (it is a lot of salt but essential for crackling). Put the meat in the hot oven for 30 minutes—by which time it should have formed crackling. Turn the oven down to 180°C (350°F/gas 4), cover the crackling with foil and continue cooking for a further 45 minutes. Turn the oven down to 150°C (300°F/gas 2).

Remove the pork from the oven and let it rest for 30 minutes. Tap off the salt. If the edges are a bit dark, trim with a knife. Cut the meat into six even slices, making sure there is some crackling on each. Place on an oven tray covered with greaseproof paper, and return it to the oven for 7 minutes. Remove from the oven, place on paper towels, remove the string and serve.

TIME 3 HOURS • SERVES 6

Goat (or lamb) cooked this way becomes meltingly tender, but it's important not to overcook the egg sauce. You want a creamy sauce, not a scramble. For maximum tenderness, you should ask your butcher for meat from a kid that weighs less than 4 kilograms (8 lb 6 oz). If the butcher can't find any goat, then baby lamb does almost as well. You could attempt to chop it up yourself but I think it's easier to ask the butcher to do it. Tell him you need 12 pieces, each about the size of a bread roll, so that each guest receives three healthy chunks. Serve this with a rocket salad.

16. Capretto con piselli
Casserole of baby goat with peas

2 large white onions, thinly sliced

6 tbsp olive oil

1.5 kg (3 lb) baby kid (or lamb), cut into about 12 pieces

250 ml (8 fl oz) white wine

400 g (13 oz) shelled fresh peas (or frozen)

3 eggs

50 g (1¾ oz) freshly grated parmesan cheese

1 tbsp chopped parsley, plus extra for serving

salt and freshly ground black pepper

In a large heavy-based casserole, sauté the onions in the olive oil over medium heat until golden, about 5 minutes. Add the meat and brown for about another 5 minutes. Add the wine, stir and boil until the liquid reduces by half, another 5 minutes.

Reduce the heat and add 200 ml (6½ fl oz) of warm water. Cover and simmer gently for about 45 minutes, until the meat is tender. Lift the lid to check it occasionally; add a little more water if the meat looks to be drying out.

After the meat has been simmering for about 40 minutes, cook the peas in boiling water for 5 minutes. (If you are using frozen peas, omit this step.) Strain and add them to the casserole and cook for another 5 minutes.

Beat the eggs in a bowl with the parmesan, parsley, salt and pepper. Pour the mixture over the meat and stir over medium heat for 1 minute, until the egg mixture starts to thicken and coats the pieces of goat. Taste and season with more salt and pepper if necessary. Sprinkle with more parsley and serve.

TIME 1 HOUR 15 MINUTES • SERVES 4

Yes, these are stinging nettles, so handle them with gloves until they are boiled—at which point they become sharp and delicious and the perfect counterpoint to plump spatchcock. The season for nettles is winter. If you want to make this dish at other times of the year, or you are nervous about being stung you could substitute English spinach. Ask the butcher to tunnel bone the spatchcocks. Serve with mashed potatoes or polenta.

17. Galletto ripieni con ortiche
Spatchcock with nettle stuffing

4 spatchcocks, size no. 4, tunnel
  boned
60 ml (2 fl oz) red wine

FOR THE STUFFING
200 g (6½ oz) nettles (or English
  spinach)
1 medium onion, finely chopped
4 tbsp unsalted butter
100 g (3½ oz) white bread, about
  2 slices
50 ml (1¾ fl oz) milk
30 g (1 oz) walnuts, roughly
  chopped
salt and freshly ground black
  pepper

Preheat the oven to 200°C (400°F/gas 6). To make the stuffing, use gloves when handling the nettles: wash them and discard the stems. Put the leaves in a saucepan of boiling water and cook for 5 minutes, strain, then chop and set aside. In a frying pan, sauté the onion in 2 tablespoons of the butter over medium heat for 10 minutes. Cut the crusts off the pieces of bread, break them into pieces and soak in the milk. After 5 minutes, squeeze out the milk and throw the bread into the pan with the onion, along with the chopped walnuts and the nettles. Season with a little salt and pepper, stir and the stuffing is ready.

Divide the stuffing into four portions. Push a portion of stuffing into each spatchcock and close the ends with toothpicks. Rub the spatchcocks with the remaining butter and place them on a baking tray. Roast them in the preheated oven for 20 minutes.

To serve, place a spatchcock on each serving plate. Stir the red wine into the roasting juices left in the baking tray and let the sauce thicken over medium heat on top of the stove for 5 minutes. Taste for salt, and pour the sauce over or around the spatchcocks.

TIME 55 MINUTES • SERVES 4

Here is the perfectionist's version of this recipe—but you could replace the venison *jus* with beef stock. It is perfect for a grand dinner party. You need to have everything ready, then at the last minute cook the gnocchi and the meat (which only takes about 5 minutes).

18. Cervo alla valtellina
Medallions of venison with pureed beetroot and pumpkin gnocchi

400 g (13 oz) venison backstrap
olive oil for frying

FOR THE VENISON JUS
100 ml (3½ fl oz) olive oil
1 onion, chopped
1 carrot, chopped
½ stick celery, chopped
1 kg (2 lb) venison bones
20 juniper berries

FOR THE MARINADE
5 cloves garlic, flattened
20 juniper berries, flattened
400 ml (13 fl oz) olive oil

FOR THE BEETROOT PUREE
6 large beetroot
1 granny smith apple, peeled,
   cored and diced
75 g (2½ oz) unsalted butter
250 ml (8 fl oz) white wine
5 cloves
1 tbsp redcurrant jelly
salt

FOR THE PUMPKIN GNOCCHI
500 g (1 lb) pumpkin
300 g (10 oz) flour
80 g (2½ oz) unsalted butter
5 sage leaves
salt

Make the *jus* (best done the day before) in the way described on page 30. If you can't find venison bones, replace the *jus* with 200 ml (6½ fl oz) of beef stock. To make the marinade, gently flatten the garlic cloves and juniper berries with the flat of a knife. Marinate the venison for 6 hours or overnight in the garlic, juniper berries and olive oil.

To make the puree, clean and trim the beetroot. Place the whole beetroot in a large saucepan and cover with water. Bring to the boil and cook until tender, about 1 hour. Strain and let the beetroot cool, then peel and slice thinly. Place the diced apple, butter, wine and cloves in a saucepan, cover and stew gently for 20 minutes, then stir in the redcurrant jelly. Add the beetroot to the apple mixture and puree; season with salt to taste.

To make the gnocchi, cut the pumpkin into pieces and take off the skin. Place the pumpkin pieces in the top of a steamer and cook until soft, about 20 minutes. Mash and season with salt. On a benchtop, make a well of the flour and put the pumpkin in the middle. Gather them together and knead with your hands until the dough is elastic. Roll the dough into a cylinder about 1 cm (½ inch) thick, then cut into pieces 1 cm (½ inch) long.

When you're nearly ready to serve the dish, add a little salt then the gnocchi to a large saucepan of boiling water and cook until the gnocchi rise to the surface, about 5 minutes. While the gnocchi are cooking, melt the butter in a frying pan, add the sage and sauté for 2 minutes. Add the drained gnocchi and sauté in the butter and sage for about 3 minutes. Reheat the venison *jus* (or beef stock).

To cook the venison, heat a little olive oil in a heavy-based frying pan. When the oil is hot, put in the whole piece of venison and brown on all sides, turning often, for about 5 minutes. Cut the meat into 1 cm (½ inch) slices and layer them down the centre of each plate, overlapping each other. Pour over about 3 tablespoons of *jus*. Make a strip of beetroot puree on one side of the meat and pumpkin gnocchi on the other side.

TIME 12 HOURS, INCLUDING MARINATING • SERVES 8

The chocolate in this cake comes in three forms: a sponge, a mousse and a ganache topping. Serve the cake with a compote of fresh berries and a scoop of ice-cream or a homemade semifreddo. Hazelnut paste is available at specialist food stores and health food shops.

19. Cioccolato verona
Chocolate layer cake

FOR THE SPONGE
5 eggs
150 g (5 oz) caster sugar
30 g (1 oz) cocoa
120 g (4 oz) flour
30 g (1 oz) melted butter

FOR THE SYRUP
100 g (3½ oz) sugar
50 ml (1¾ fl oz) Amaretto liqueur

FOR THE MOUSSE
½ sheet gelatine
20 g (¾ oz) sugar
60 g (2 oz) chocolate (70 per cent cocoa), broken into pieces
1 tsp hazelnut paste
100 ml (3½ fl oz) cream

FOR THE GANACHE
100 ml (3½ fl oz) cream
100 g (3½ oz) chocolate (70 per cent cocoa), broken into pieces

FOR THE COMPOTE
200 g (6½ oz) mixed berries, whatever is in season
1 tbsp sugar
½ tsp rosewater
2 tsp grenadine

1 x 20-cm (8-inch) round springform cake tin

Preheat the oven to 180°C (350°F/gas 4). Butter the cake tin and line it with buttered greaseproof paper. Beat the eggs and the sugar together until light and thick. Sift the cocoa and flour together and fold them gently into the egg mixture. Pour in the melted butter. Gently pour the batter into the cake tin and even out the top. Bake in the preheated oven until springy and coming away from the sides of the tin, about 30 minutes. Turn out the sponge onto a rack and let it cool for 15 minutes. Then slice the top off the sponge to even it out and cut the crust off the sides. Line the cake tin with greaseproof paper and put the trimmed sponge back in.

While the cake is baking, make the syrup and mousse. For the syrup, boil the sugar with 100 ml (3½ fl oz) of water in a saucepan until the sugar has dissolved. Cool and add the Amaretto. Soak the sponge with the syrup. To make the mousse, soak the gelatine in cold water for 2 minutes, then squeeze to remove excess water. Put the sugar into a saucepan with 30 ml (1 fl oz) of water and bring to the boil. Turn down to a low heat, add the gelatine and let it dissolve—do not allow it to boil. Add the chocolate and stir until it has melted. Finally, add the hazelnut paste and continue stirring until smooth, about 1 minute. Remove the pan from the heat and cool. Whip the cream into stiff peaks and gently fold it into the mixture. Spread the mousse evenly over the sponge, levelling it off with a palette knife. Put the sponge into the freezer for 2 hours.

To make the ganache, in a small saucepan bring the cream to the boil, remove from the heat and stir in the chocolate until smooth. Leave to rest. When the ganache is lukewarm, take the sponge out of the freezer and tin; put it on a rack with a plate underneath. Gently pour the sauce over the sponge, working from the centre to the edge and letting it drip onto the plate underneath. If you want to, decorate it with squares of edible gold leaf. Put the cake in the fridge (not the freezer) for at least 1 hour.

For the compote, cut up the berries, sprinkle with the sugar, rosewater and grenadine and let them macerate for 15 minutes. Distribute the compote around each slice of cake and serve.

TIME 4 HOURS • SERVES 4

Unlike most of the recipes in the book, this serves eight because it would be absurd to go to all the trouble of making it for only four. And you will certainly want to have a few slices left over for the next day (it will last for up to five days in the fridge). At one level this is the simplest recipe in the book because it involves only two ingredients—apples and sugar (plus cream and ginger for serving). But there are two other equally vital ingredients—time and care.

20. Mille mele
Baked apple cake

2.5 kg (5 lb) golden delicious
    apples, peeled and cored
juice of 1 lemon
1 kg (2 lb) sugar
300 ml (10 fl oz) cream
20 g (¾ oz) fresh ginger, grated

1 x 25-cm (10-inch) diameter
    springform cake tin
2 x deep-sided baking trays

Preheat the oven to 180°C (350°F/gas 4). Slice the apples as thinly as you can—use a mandolin if you have one; if you don't, use the sharpest knife in your kitchen. As you cut the slices, put them in a bowl of water into which you have squeezed the juice of a lemon; as you assemble the *mille mele*, dry the apple slices on paper towels.

Cover the base of the cake tin with a layer of apple slices, overlapping them in a circular pattern. Sprinkle on some sugar, and then cover with another layer of slices, then more sugar and so on. When you have layered about a quarter of the apples, press down hard on them with your hands, squeezing the layers together; do this again when you have used up about three-quarters of the apple slices. Build into a mound of apple and sugar that extends about 1 cm (½ inch) above the top of the tin.

Sit the cake tin on a rack in a deep-side baking tray and place in the preheated oven; bake for 30 minutes. Have a second baking tray ready. Remove the tray from the oven and, using oven gloves, lift the cake tin and rack out of the tray and put them into the other tray. A lot of juice will have run down into the first baking tray—pour that juice over the mound of apples in the cake tin; set the first tray aside (you don't need to wash it). Bake the cake for another 1½ hours, every 15 minutes swapping the two baking trays over and pouring the juice in the bottom of the trays over the apples.

By this time the 'cake' should be dark brown and slightly firm on top. Let it to cool for 15 minutes. Pour any syrup remaining in the baking trays over the cake. (If the syrup's very runny, put it in a saucepan over medium heat and reduce until it's thickened.) Cut as many slices as you need for your guests. Whip the cream and fold in the freshly grated ginger and serve with the *mille mele*.

TIME 2 HOURS 30 MINUTES • SERVES 8

The Italian name for this translates as 'a thousand leaves' but, to be honest, I've cut it back to just three leaves of pastry and three leaves of sponge, between which are strawberries and *crema pasticceria*, a delicious kind of egg custard. I'll forgive you for not making your own puff pastry. You can buy perfectly good frozen puff pastry at most supermarkets, but make sure that it has been made with butter.

21. Millefoglie
Puff pastry with strawberries and hazelnuts

2 sheets puff pastry, frozen
250 ml (8 fl oz) cream
50 g (1¾ oz) icing sugar
400 g (13 oz) strawberries,
    quartered lengthways
300 g (10 oz) hazelnuts, peeled,
    roasted and crushed

FOR THE SYRUP
250 g (8 oz) sugar
50 ml (1¾ fl oz) Strega (or other
    liqueur to your taste)

FOR THE SPONGE
5 eggs
150 g (5 oz) sugar
150 g (5 oz) flour
30 g (1 oz) butter, melted

FOR THE CREMA PASTICCERIA
1 litre (35 fl oz) milk
1½ vanilla beans, split
12 egg yolks
250 g (8 oz) caster sugar
80 g (2½ oz) cornflour

1 x 20-cm (8-inch) diameter
    springform cake tin
1 x 8-cm (3-inch) diameter metal
    cutter
1 x piping bag

Preheat the oven to 180°C (350°F/gas 4). Prepare the cake tin: butter its base and sides and line it with buttered greaseproof paper. For the syrup, boil together the sugar, Strega and 250 ml (8 fl oz) of water. Set aside.

To make the sponge, whisk the eggs and sugar until they are thick and creamy. Sift the flour and gently fold in, along with the melted butter. Pour the mixture into the prepared cake tin. Bake in the preheated oven for approximately 30 minutes, until firm to the touch. Remove the cake from the tin and cool on a rack.

To make the *crema pasticceria*, place the milk and split vanilla beans in a heavy-based saucepan and bring to the boil. Meanwhile, whisk the egg yolks and sugar in a large bowl until well combined, then add the cornflour and mix well. Slowly whisk the boiled milk into the egg mixture until well combined.

Pour the mixture back into the saucepan and cook, uncovered, over medium heat, whisking vigorously until the mixture just begins to bubble, about 2–3 minutes. Turn the heat down to low and continue whisking for a further 2 minutes (the mixture will thicken rapidly). Pour into a shallow dish and place plastic wrap directly on top of the *crema* to prevent a skin forming. Allow to cool, then chill in the fridge.

To make the pastry 'leaves', defrost the pastry sheets, but not completely; the sheets must remain cold. Roll each sheet out to a thickness of about 2.5 mm (⅛ inch). Place a sheet of greaseproof paper on a baking tray, lay the pastry sheets over the paper and prick the pastry with a fork. Put another sheet of greaseproof paper on top and weigh it down with a second baking tray to prevent the pastry from rising unevenly. Bake in the preheated oven for 10–15 minutes until the pastry is golden. Leave it to cool on a rack.

RECIPE CONTINUES ON PAGE 165

To assemble the *millefoglie*, cut 12 discs out of the pastry sheets using the metal cutter. With the same cutter, cut out four circles of sponge 1 cm (½ inch) high. Place one of the pastry discs on a board, top with a disc of sponge and brush with sugar syrup, making sure the sponge is completely moistened. Using a piping bag, pipe the *crema pasticceria* onto the sponge in a spiral pattern. Arrange four pieces of strawberries on top of the *crema*, cover with a layer of pastry, then more *crema* and strawberries as above, finishing with a disc of pastry. You should have three pastry layers. Repeat the process for the other three *millefoglie*.

Whisk together the cream and icing sugar until they form stiff peaks. Carefully cover the sides of the cakes with the whipped cream, then roll in the hazelnuts and dust the top with icing sugar. Serve with the remaining strawberries scattered around the *millefoglie*.

TIME 1 HOUR 20 MINUTES • SERVES 4

At the end of every dinner at Buon Ricordo, I give my guests little treats with coffee. You could serve these at your spectacular dinner party or as part of an afternoon tea. The word *chiacchiere* is pronounced 'key-uck-yeah-reh'. Saying it out loud sounds like what it means—'chattering'.

22. Chiacchiere
Cinnamon pastries

100 g (3½ oz) unsalted butter
350 g (11½ oz) flour
3 eggs
2 pinches of salt
olive oil for frying
300 g (10 oz) icing sugar
1 tbsp ground cinnamon

Leave the butter out of the fridge for an hour so that it softens. Place the flour on a large board or benchtop, make a well in the centre and break the eggs into it. Add the butter and salt and mix it all together with your hands. Knead the dough until it becomes smooth and silky. Shape it into a ball, wrap in plastic wrap and leave it to rest for an hour in the fridge.

Sprinkle some flour onto the board and work the dough with a rolling pin until it is a wide rectangle about 2.5 mm (⅛ inch) thick. Cut out diamond shapes about 4 cm (1½ inches) long.

In a deep frying pan or wok, heat 6 cm (2½ inches) of olive oil until it sizzles when a drop of water is thrown in. Place the diamond-shaped dough into the oil, frying a small number each time. Remove them when they are golden and puffy, about 2 minutes. Drain on paper towels. While they are still hot, toss the *chiacchiere* with the icing sugar and cinnamon.

TIME 1 HOUR 15 MINUTES • MAKES ABOUT 20

5

hearty health

One of the many great things about Italian cooking is that most of it is pretty good for you—without even trying to be. And many of its best dishes are vegetarian—without even trying to be. Trial and error over millennia of living close to the land have given Italians a taste for, and a talent with, ingredients that don't clog the blood or strain the heart or stress the digestive system. Research done by American heart surgeons found that Italians had one of the lowest rates of strokes and heart attacks in the world.

This chapter is full of lighter meals you can eat every day rather than the richer and more elaborate meals you keep for special occasions. This does not imply you would only want to cook these recipes out of duty. Pleasure is just as important with everyday eating. I proudly serve most of these dishes in my restaurant to customers who are reckless about their bodies. They'd be shocked to learn I might be doing them some good.

If you're keen to play down fats or sugars or meats in your diet and still have fun at the table, you'll find inspiration here.

Since we're discussing particular preferences, let me take the opportunity to guide you through this book. If you or your guests are vegan, you'll have no trouble with the linguine with mushrooms (recipe #5 in this chapter), the chickpea salad (#7) and the fennel and radicchio salad (#8). In other chapters, you'll enjoy pasta with the Napoletana sauce on page 20 and the bruschetta on the same page, the fig salad on page 29, the cabbage with chilli on page 24, the big pizza on page 42 (without the cheese, of course), the zucchini flowers on page 44, the blood orange salad on page 47, the tomato and pear salad by itself on page 51, the four little pastas on pages 54 to 57 (without the cheese and ham), the lime granita and the peaches in red wine on page 71, the stuffed artichokes on page 88 (minus the parmesan) and the potato and olive tortino on page 133 (minus the anchovies).

If you're a vegetarian, or following a kosher diet, you'll embrace these recipes in this chapter: the artichoke and fennel salad (#1); the eggplant with oriental sauce (#2); the lentil soup (#3) leaving out the bacon; the spinach and cavolo nero soup (#4) using vegetable stock instead of chicken stock; and the Christmas salad (#6) without the anchovies.

And if you're a fish eater who wants to avoid meat, in this chapter you could go for any of the above, or the calamari with peas (#9), the bonito with raw vegetables (#10), one fish, three dishes (#11), the groper with roast fennel (#12), scampi with white peaches (#13), snapper with Tuscan bread salad (#14), the snapper in pizza dough (#15), the goldband snapper with zucchini flowers (#16), ocean trout with tomato and lemon zest (#17), the stuffed peaches (#20), and the mixed berry pizza (#21). Plus the many other seafood dishes throughout the book.

1. **Finocchiara** Fennel and raw globe artichoke salad

2. **Melanzane con coriandolo** Eggplant with oriental sauce

3. **Zuppa di lenticchie** Lentil soup

4. **Zuppa alla montanara** Spinach and cavolo nero soup

5. **Linguine con funghi** Linguine with chestnut mushrooms

6. **Insalata di rinforzo** Christmas salad

7. **Ceci farciti** Chickpea salad

8. **Insalata di finocchio e radicchio** Fennel and radicchio salad

9. **Calamari con pomodori** Calamari with tomatoes and peas

10. **Sarda marinata** Marinated bonito with raw vegetables

11. **Un pesce, tre piatti** One fish, three dishes

12. **Cernia con finocchio al forno** Groper with roast fennel and tomato

13. **Pesce con pesche** Scampi with white peaches

14. **Orata con panzanella rivisitata** Snapper with Tuscan bread salad

15. **Orata in crosta di pane** Whole snapper in pizza dough

16. **Pagello con fiori** Goldband snapper with zucchini flowers

17. **Trota salmonata primavera** Ocean trout with tomato and lemon zest

18. **Quaglie al mosto** Grilled quails with apple and walnut salad

19. **Vitello con salsa di rucola e barbabietole** Roast veal with rocket sauce and beetroot

20. **Pesche ripiene** Poached peaches

21. **Pizza di Natale** Mixed berry 'pizza'

At the right time of year—winter—you don't need to cook globe artichokes. Raw is beautiful. The small ones have a delicious fresh flavour when sliced thinly and served with fennel and parmesan. The 'cooking' is done by the lemon marinade.

1. Finocchiara

Fennel and raw globe artichoke salad

3 globe artichokes
juice of 1 lemon, plus 1 tbsp
2 fennel bulbs
4 tbsp extra virgin olive oil
100 g (3½ oz) parmesan cheese, shaved
1 tbsp finely chopped parsley
salt and freshly ground black pepper

Clean the artichokes. Remove the stem and cut one-third off the top. Cut the artichoke in half and scrap out any coarse choke (although there should not be much if the artichoke is fresh and young). Slice very thinly. Marinate immediately in the juice of a lemon or else the artichokes will oxidise and blacken. Leave for 30 minutes.

Meanwhile, remove the outer layer from the fennel. Cut the bulbs in half. Remove the hard cores at the bottom and discard them. Slice the fennel into thin layers.

Drain the lemon juice from the sliced artichokes. In a bowl, mix together the artichokes and fennel. Add salt and pepper to taste and the extra virgin olive oil and the 1 tablespoon of lemon juice. Toss well. Divide the mixture among four plates and shave some parmesan on top. Sprinkle with parsley and drizzle with a little more extra virgin olive oil.

TIME 50 MINUTES • SERVES 4

Melanzane con coriandolo tastes even better a day after you make it. Don't say coriander is not Italian—the ancient Romans used it and that's good enough for me. They may also have used eggplant. I make no such claims about mirin, a sweet Japanese cooking wine.

2. Melanzane con coriandolo
Eggplant with oriental sauce

125 ml (4 fl oz) white balsamic
   vinegar (medium sweet)
60 ml (2 fl oz) mirin
3 tbsp extra virgin olive oil
1 clove garlic, roughly chopped
4 large eggplants
leaves of 4 sprigs coriander, roughly
   chopped
salt and freshly ground black
   pepper

In a bowl, mix the balsamic, mirin, extra virgin olive oil and garlic and let the mixture rest for 1 hour. Peel the eggplants and cut them into slices 2 cm (¾ inch) thick. Steam the eggplant slices in a large covered saucepan with 4 tablespoons of water for 8 minutes. Dry the eggplant slices on paper towels, then place them on a large serving platter.

Strain the sauce and discard the pieces of garlic. Beat the mixture until it emulsifies. Season to taste and pour it over the eggplant. Sprinkle over the coriander. Leave the dish in the fridge for 30 minutes before serving.

TIME 1 HOUR 30 MINUTES, INCLUDING CHILLING • SERVES 4

In Italy the best lentils come from an area called Castelluccio, in Umbria. I've found similar lentils from the Grampians in Victoria. They are so small they need very little soaking. If you can't get the small slate green lentils, soak larger lentils for 2 hours.

3. Zuppa di lenticchie
Lentil soup

160 g (5½ oz) lentils, soaked
2 medium red onions, finely
   chopped
3 tbsp olive oil
2 carrots, chopped
1 stick celery, chopped
200 g (6½ oz) smoked bacon, cut
   into 4 chunks (optional)
2 roma tomatoes, chopped
1 tbsp fresh thyme leaves
extra virgin olive oil for serving
salt and freshly ground black
   pepper

If you are using large lentils, soak them for 2 hours. Place the onions in a large saucepan with the olive oil and sauté over medium heat until translucent, about 5 minutes. Add the carrots and celery to the pan and cook for another 5 minutes. If you are using it, add the bacon pieces at this point and sauté them along with the celery.

Add the lentils, stir for a couple of minutes, then add 1 litre (35 fl oz) of warm water. Bring to the boil, then reduce the heat and simmer uncovered for 30 minutes. Add the chopped tomatoes and the thyme. Cook for a further 10 minutes, adding extra water if the soup seems to be too thick. Season with salt and pepper to taste. Serve drizzled with a little extra virgin olive oil.

TIME 3 HOURS, INCLUDING SOAKING • SERVES 4

The Italian name for this *zuppa* translates as 'mountaineer's soup'. The recipe comes from the north of Italy, where they need such sustenance to build their strength for climbing. There are big mountains near Naples—you've heard of Vesuvius, I dare say—so we southerners feel entitled to make this soup too. In the north they tend to add pork fat, but my mother made a lighter version.

4. Zuppa alla montanara
Spinach and cavolo nero soup

400 g (13 oz) dried cannellini
   beans
1.5 litres (52 fl oz) chicken broth
   (see recipe, page 53)
500 g (1 lb) cavolo nero
400 g (13 oz) English spinach
4 slices Italian bread, about 2 cm
   (¾ inch) thick
a little olive oil
1 clove garlic, peeled
4 tbsp freshly grated parmesan
   cheese
salt and freshly ground black
   pepper

Soak the cannellini beans for at least 6 hours, drain off the water then put them in a large saucepan with more water. Bring to the boil and simmer for 20 minutes. Drain, then return the beans to the pan and add the chicken broth. Bring to the boil.

Prepare the cavolo nero: cut off the stems and wash well (sometimes they are a little gritty), then roughly chop. Add to the broth and simmer for 15 minutes. Wash the spinach well, remove the stems and cut in half. Put the spinach in the broth and cook for a further 15 minutes. Season to taste with salt and pepper.

Meanwhile, preheat the oven to 200°C (400°F/gas 6). Brush the bread with olive oil and rub with the garlic. Toast on an open flame so they char slightly, then bake in the preheated oven for 5 minutes. Cut the toasted bread into large cubes to make crostini. Ladle the soup into bowls, sprinkle with the grated parmesan and top each bowl with four crostini.

TIME 6 HOURS 45 MINUTES, INCLUDING SOAKING ● SERVES 4

One of my fondest childhood memories is my grandfather making this wonderful dish with the long thin mushrooms we called *chiodini* (nails). All my adult life I have tried to recreate the amazing flavour he was able to achieve and this is the nearest I have come to it. Those *chiodini* don't grow in Australia, but I've found that a mixture of chestnut mushrooms (for texture) and shiitake mushrooms (for flavour) comes close when combined with a little chilli. You can substitute your other favourite mushrooms. But if it's a time of year when all you can find are button mushrooms, don't bother trying this. Sautéing the mushrooms takes only a few minutes, while the pasta is cooking, so this is an easy, fast dish.

5. Linguine con funghi
Linguine with chestnut mushrooms

150 g (5 oz) chestnut mushrooms
150 g (5 oz) shiitake mushrooms
400 g (13 oz) linguine
5 tbsp olive oil
1 small red chilli, finely chopped
3 cloves garlic, finely sliced
2 tomatoes, peeled and diced
    (optional)
2 tbsp finely chopped parsley
salt

If the mushrooms are big, cut them in half lengthways. Add salt to a large saucepan of boiling water and throw in the linguine. Cook until almost *al dente*, about 5 minutes, and drain.

Meanwhile, put the olive oil, chilli and garlic in a large frying pan and sauté over medium heat until the garlic is light golden, about 1 minute. Add the mushrooms and toss for about 4 minutes. Some people like to toss a few diced tomatoes into the mushrooms at this point. Turn the heat up to high and throw the linguine into the frying pan. Stir the mushrooms through the pasta for about a minute. Add salt to taste and sprinkle over the chopped parsley. Toss thoroughly and serve immediately. There's no need for parmesan with this.

TIME 15 MINUTES • SERVES 4

It's the colour contrasts I love about this salad as much as the flavour contrasts. The brightness of the red and white would be a good enough reason to call it a Christmas food, but it's also the dish we traditionally eat in Naples on Christmas Eve. The Italian name includes the word *rinforzo*, which means 'reinforcement', or body building, and also implies that you can keep reinforcing the leftovers with new ingredients if you're feeling a little peckish on Boxing Day.

6. Insalata di rinforzo
Christmas salad

500 ml (16 fl oz) white vinegar
1 medium cauliflower, divided into florets
2 carrots, sliced into rounds
1 yellow capsicum, cut into 1-cm (½-inch) wide strips
1 red capsicum, cut into 1-cm (½-inch) wide strips
20 small cornichon gherkins
20 small white pickled onions
1 handful black olives, pitted
4 tbsp extra virgin olive oil
8 anchovies in oil, drained and chopped
salt

Put the vinegar in a large saucepan with 1 litre (35 fl oz) of water and bring to the boil. Add the cauliflower and cook for about 12 minutes. Scoop out the cauliflower (retaining the cooking water to use for the carrots and capsicums), drain it and put it into a salad bowl. Set aside in the fridge.

Add the carrots to the saucepan and cook for 10 minutes, scoop them out, drain and add them to the bowl with the cauliflower. Put the bowl back in the fridge. Cook the capsicums in the boiling water for 5 minutes, drain and add to the salad bowl. Return the bowl to the fridge for 10 minutes.

Add the whole gherkins, pickled onions and olives to the bowl. Season with salt to taste and dress generously with the extra virgin olive oil. Sprinkle with the anchovies. Leave the salad to marinate in the fridge for at least 12 hours before serving.

TIME 12 HOURS 45 MINUTES, INCLUDING MARINATING • SERVES 4

Ceci farciti literally means 'stuffed chickpeas', which you should not attempt. More important is to know the pronunciation of the Italian name: 'chech-ee far-cheet-ee'. In 1282 a bunch of Sicilians staged a revolt against their French conquerors, and slaughtered anyone in the streets who could not pronounce the word for chickpea—the French pronounced it 'sesee'. Let that be a lesson to you.

7. Ceci farciti
Chickpea salad

300 g (10 oz) dried chickpeas
1 handful of celery leaves, chopped
3 stalks celery, white part only,
    chopped 1 cm (½ inch) thick
3 small carrots, sliced into rounds
    1 cm (½ inch) thick
125 ml (4 fl oz) extra virgin olive oil
juice of 1 lemon
salt and freshly ground black pepper

Soak the chickpeas for at least 6 hours. Drain, then place them in a large saucepan, cover with water and bring to the boil. Simmer until tender, about 75 minutes, adding more water if they look like drying out. Strain them and cool.

Put the celery leaves in a salad bowl. Add the celery stalks, chickpeas and carrots. Mix the olive oil and lemon juice, pour over the chickpeas and season to taste with salt and pepper.

TIME 7 HOURS 40 MINUTES, INCLUDING SOAKING • SERVES 4

The best deep red radicchio is available in winter time, as is the best fennel, so there's not a lot of point in trying to serve this in summer. It's a great palate cleanser after a meaty pasta or some roasted meat.

8. Insalata di finocchio e radicchio
Fennel and radicchio salad

1 radicchio
2 fennel bulbs
1 tbsp extra virgin olive oil
1 tsp balsamic vinegar
salt and freshly ground black pepper

Break the radicchio into small pieces. Clean the fennel bulbs, removing the outer layers and core at the bottom, then slice them into strips 5 mm (¼ inch) thick. Place in a salad bowl with the radicchio leaves and season with salt and pepper to taste.

Mix together the extra virgin olive oil and balsamic vinegar. Pour over the salad, toss well and serve.

TIME 5 MINUTES • SERVES 4

This dish works as an antipasto or as a sauce for pasta. The best pasta to use would be linguine, which you cook for about 6 minutes until it's still firm, drain, and toss into the frying pan with the calamari and tomatoes so that it finishes its cooking by absorbing some of the delicious juices. You can also serve this with small pieces of toast or slices of baked polenta.

9. Calamari con pomodori
Calamari with tomatoes and peas

2 small calamari, cleaned
2 cloves garlic
6 tbsp olive oil
500 ml (16 fl oz) white wine
200 g (6½ oz) shelled fresh peas
1 small red chilli, seeded and finely
   chopped (optional)
16 cherry tomatoes, halved
2 tbsp finely chopped parsley
salt and freshly ground black
   pepper

Wash the calamari, cut off the tentacles and reserve (they are the tastiest part). Cut the rest into rings about 5 mm (¼ inch) wide.

Thump a clove of garlic with the palm of your hand or press down on it with the flat of a knife, peel off the skin and put it in a frying pan with 3 tablespoons of the olive oil. Sauté over medium heat until it's golden, about 2 minutes. Throw in the calamari rings and tentacles and sauté for 2 minutes, then add the white wine, bring to the boil and simmer gently over moderate heat for 10 minutes. Remove and discard the garlic clove.

In a saucepan, boil the peas in salted water until tender, about 8 minutes, then drain.

Chop the remaining clove of garlic, then sauté it in the cleaned frying pan in the remaining olive oil for 2 minutes, with the chopped chilli if using. Add the cherry tomatoes to the pan and cook gently for 2 more minutes. Add the calamari and peas, stir and simmer uncovered over low heat for 10 minutes. Season to taste with salt and pepper. Pile onto a serving dish and sprinkle over the parsley.

TIME 40 MINUTES • SERVES 4

Here's a perfect summer fish dish, of invigorating sharpness. The Italian name *sarda* makes bonito sound like a sardine and, indeed, bonito is of that family, although it is milder tasting. The vinegary flavour of the fish is balanced here by the waxy potatoes. This dish is served at room temperature.

10. Sarda marinata
Marinated bonito with raw vegetables

4 x 180 g (6 oz) bonito fillets
12 small waxy potatoes

FOR THE MARINADE
200 ml (6½ fl oz) white wine
    vinegar
2 medium carrots, finely sliced
2 sticks celery, finely sliced
2 red onions, finely sliced
200 ml (6½ fl oz) extra virgin
    olive oil
salt and freshly ground black
    pepper

Place the bonito fillets on a tray. For the marinade, bring the vinegar and 200 ml (6½ fl oz) of water to the boil, add the carrots and celery and boil for 4 minutes. Pour this over the bonito and let it marinate for 10 minutes, then remove the bonito. Strain, discarding the liquid and keeping the vegetables, and put the bonito back on the tray. Add the onions to the carrots and celery, stirring to mix well, and heap the vegetables around the bonito. Pour the extra virgin olive oil over the fish, cover with plastic wrap and leave in the fridge to marinate for 12 hours. Take the tray out of the fridge 30 minutes before serving.

Boil the potatoes for 15 minutes, let them cool a little, then peel. To serve, place three warm potatoes on each plate and flatten them slightly with your palm. Place one piece of fish and 3 tablespoons of marinade on top of the potatoes on each plate. Season to taste.

TIME 12 HOURS 30 MINUTES, INCLUDING MARINATING ● SERVES 4

Here's one of the rare cases where a name sounds more poetic in English than in Italian. I use a whole fish to create three courses, so all that's missing is the dessert. I invented this in the spirit of the times when we need to learn to maximise our resources and not waste anything. I've suggested using a whole ocean perch, but any smooth-fleshed fish that is suitable for sushi would do. It would be fun to try it with bonito, or goldband snapper, or the long shiny creature that's called *morena* in Italy (large-head hairtail in English).

I've called the three dishes *crudo di persico* (marinated raw fish in a style some call *carpaccio*), *gnocchi alla saracena* (a fish stock with gnocchi named in honour of the Saracens, who influenced the food and architecture of my Amalfi coast) and *filetto con oregano* (fillet with wine and herbs) for the main course. I know, the last name needs more poetry.

The only ingredient that may be hard to find is the *bottarga* (dried tuna roe), which I use to garnish the *crudo*—ask for it at your delicatessen. Serve the *filetto* with a dish of boiled potatoes.

11. Un pesce, tre piatti
One fish, three dishes

1 x 1.5 kg (3 lb) ocean perch or
    similar fish, gutted and scaled
1 large onion, chopped
3 tbsp olive oil
1 large carrot, chopped
1 small stick celery, chopped
1 bay leaf

FOR THE CRUDO
1 clove garlic, finely chopped
250 ml (8 fl oz) extra virgin olive oil
juice of 1 lemon
20 g (¾ oz) *bottarga* (dried tuna roe)
1 tbsp finely chopped parsley
sea salt

FOR THE GNOCCHI
1 large loaf wholemeal bread
2 eggs
1 tbsp freshly grated parmesan
    cheese
2 cloves garlic, finely chopped
1½ tbsp chopped parsley
salt and freshly ground black
    pepper

First, prepare the fish. Cut off the head and tail, and put them aside for stock. Now remove the fillets. Using a very sharp knife, start from the top and slice along the side of the fish just above the bone to cut away the top fillet. Without turning the fish over, pull away the bones and then lift off the other fillet. Put the fillets in the fridge, covered, and keep the bones for the stock.

Now you're ready to make the stock. In a large saucepan, sauté the onion in the olive oil for 5 minutes. Add the carrot, celery and bay leaf and cook for another 5 minutes. Wash the fish head and tail thoroughly and add them, with the bones, to the saucepan. Sauté for 2 minutes, turning with a wooden spoon. Add 2 litres (72 fl oz) of water and bring to the boil, then turn down the heat and simmer the stock uncovered for 45 minutes.

While the stock is simmering, you can prepare the other two courses.

For the *crudo*, cut the bottom third of each fillet—the thinnest part of the flesh. Reserve the fatter section of the fillets for the main course; put this back in the fridge.

In a small bowl, put the finely chopped garlic and the extra virgin olive oil and stir together. Set aside while you slice the *crudo*. Place one of the thin pieces of fillet on a board, skin side down. Using a very sharp knife and cutting away from your hand, slice along the surface of the flesh as thinly as you can, cutting at least six slices from each fillet.

FOR THE FILETTO
60 ml (2 fl oz) extra virgin olive oil
1 large clove garlic, finely chopped
60 ml (2 fl oz) dry white wine
30 green olives, pitted
2 tbsp white wine vinegar
leaves of 6 sprigs oregano, chopped
salt

Divide the slices among four plates. Squeeze the lemon juice over and let the fish marinate for 10 minutes, then pour off the lemon juice and dab the slices dry with a paper towel. Sprinkle with salt and generously splash each plate with the olive oil infused with garlic. Grate a little *bottarga* over each plate and sprinkle with a little chopped parsley. Now the *crudo* is ready to serve.

Preheat the oven to 180°C (350°F/gas 4). For the gnocchi, pull the soft part out of the middle of the bread and soak the pieces in water for 5 minutes. Squeeze the water out. Beat the eggs and stir in the parmesan, garlic, 1 tablespoon of the parsley and salt and pepper to taste. Thoroughly mash the bread into the egg mixture and then, using your hands, mould the mixture into dumplings about the size of a walnut. Make about six balls for each person.

About 10 minutes before you're ready to serve the soup, strain the stock into a clean saucepan and, covered, bring it back to simmering point. Throw in the dumplings and continue boiling until the gnocchi float to the surface, about 5 minutes. Serve in soup bowls. Add salt to taste, and sprinkle on the remaining finely chopped parsley.

To cook the main course, cut each fat piece of fillet in half, so you have four pieces of fish, each with the skin still on. Put the extra virgin olive oil into an ovenproof frying pan and sauté the garlic over medium heat until golden, about 2 minutes. Put the fish into the pan and sear on both sides, about 1 minute per side. Add the white wine and olives and bring to the boil. Cover the pan with foil and place it in the preheated oven for 12 minutes. Remove the fish from the pan and keep warm while you make the sauce.

Put the pan back on top of the stove, bring the liquid to the boil and add the vinegar. Check the seasoning and add a little salt if needed, then place the fish back into the sauce to warm for 1 minute. Place the fish on serving plates, pour over some sauce and sprinkle with oregano.

TIME 1 HOUR 40 MINUTES • SERVES 4

Groper is one of the few fish with the strength of flavour to stand up to fennel, which sweetens a little when it's roasted but still retains its characteristic aniseed taste. Here I've emphasised the aniseed notes by sprinkling fennel seeds on the tomato, which is also roasted.

12. Cernia con finocchio al forno

Groper with roast fennel and tomato

2 fennel bulbs, quartered
125 ml (4 fl oz) extra virgin olive oil
4 tomatoes, halved
2 tsp fennel seeds
olive oil for frying
4 x 180 g (6 oz) groper fillets
sea salt flakes and freshly ground
    black pepper

Preheat the oven to 180°C (350°F/gas 4). Coat the cut sides of the fennel pieces with extra virgin olive oil and grind over some black pepper. Pour a little extra virgin olive oil on the cut side of the tomato halves, season with a pinch of salt and sprinkle with fennel seeds.

Cover the bottom of an ovenproof frying pan with a thin film of olive oil, place over medium heat and sear the fish fillets for a minute on each side. Add the fennel and tomatoes to the fish and put the pan into the preheated oven for 15 minutes.

To serve, put a piece of fish, two tomato halves and a piece of fennel on each plate. Drizzle a little extra virgin olive oil around the plate and sprinkle the fish with a few flakes of sea salt.

TIME 25 MINUTES • SERVES 4

All right, the Italian title is another word game. It's pronounced 'pesh-eh con pes-kay', and literally translates as fish with peaches. English speakers always get in trouble when they try to order peaches or fish from Italian menus, so this title is a small language lesson. I know scampi is not a fish—it's a crustacean—but the pun is lost if you call it that in Italian.

I should point out that scampi are usually not fresh, but this doesn't matter. They are snap frozen on the fishing boat at sea. If that didn't happen, they'd be stale by the time they got to shore. Fortunately they lose no flavour in the freezing process, and I think ripe peaches lusciously enhance their sweetness.

13. Pesce con pesche
Scampi with white peaches

16 scampi
8 ripe white peaches
2 tbsp extra virgin olive oil, plus
   extra for serving
10 stalks of chives, finely chopped
salt and freshly ground black
   pepper

Preheat the oven to 200°C (400°F/gas 6). Remove the shell from the back of the scampi by cutting down the middle of the shell with strong scissors and pulling the pieces away. Make sure to remove the black string of intestinal tract. Leave the head and the tail attached to the flesh, for visual effect. Skin and cut up five of the peaches and puree them in a blender with the olive oil. Stir in a little salt and pepper and most of the chopped chives (save a teaspoonful to sprinkle over later). Peel and segment the other three peaches.

Place the scampi on a baking tray, shells down, brush with a little olive oil and put in the preheated oven. Bake for 5 minutes.

To serve, place four scampi in the middle of each plate. Divide the pieces of peach among the plates on one side of the scampi and pour the peach puree down the other side, or pour a little puree on the scampi and serve the rest separately. Drizzle with extra virgin olive oil.

TIME 20 MINUTES • SERVES 4

Italians are obsessed with bread. In the south, some people kiss bread that has gone stale before they throw it away to avoid giving offence to the 'body of Christ'. This recipe avoids that risk by using up stale bread as part of a delicious salad called *panzanella*.

This *panzanella* is 'revisited' because I have adapted it slightly from the Tuscan classic. The original often contains capsicums and anchovies, but that would be too powerful to go with a mild fish such as snapper.

14. Orata con panzanella rivisitata
Snapper with Tuscan bread salad

6 tbsp extra virgin olive oil

2 tbsp red wine vinegar

2 tbsp small capers

1 roma tomato, diced

1 handful black olives, pitted and
    chopped

½ Spanish onion, sliced

125 g (4½ oz) parsley, coarsely
    chopped

4 pieces stale bread

olive oil for frying

4 x 180 g (6 oz) snapper fillets

salt and freshly ground black
    pepper

Preheat the oven to 200°C (400°F/gas 6). Mix together the extra virgin olive oil and vinegar. Soak the capers in cold water for a few minutes until the salt is washed off, then drain them. Place the tomato, olives, capers, onion and parsley in a salad bowl, pour over the oil and vinegar dressing and season with salt and freshly ground black pepper to taste. Set aside for 30 minutes.

To make breadcrumbs, bake the slices of bread in the preheated oven until crunchy, about 15 minutes. Then break the bread into small fragments and set aside.

Put a little olive oil in a non-stick frying pan and place over medium heat. Add the snapper fillets, skin side down, and cook for 2 minutes on each side.

Just before serving, stir the breadcrumbs through the salad. Divide the salad among four plates and place a piece of fish on top of each.

TIME 30 MINUTES • SERVES 4

What's a pizza doing in a chapter that is supposed to be healthy, I hear you asking. Answer: it's not being eaten. Here the dough forms a crust around the fish to seal in its juices. Once its job is done, the pizza gets thrown away. And the tomatoes that might have been on the pizza are served as a sauce flavoured with fresh thyme. This is a very old recipe from Naples, but only a few restaurants still make it these days.

Serve the fish with a mixed green leaf salad. Dress it by first squeezing on the juice of half a lemon, then toss before adding 60 ml (2 fl oz) of extra virgin olive oil and a sprinkle of salt.

15. Orata in crosta di pane
Whole snapper in pizza dough

1 clove garlic, peeled and finely
  sliced
2 x 400 g (13 oz) whole snappers,
  scaled and gutted
2 x quantities of pizza dough (see
  recipe, page 41)

FOR THE SAUCE
4 roma tomatoes, peeled, seeded
  and diced
4 tbsp extra virgin olive oil
2 tbsp thyme leaves
salt

To make the sauce, put the tomatoes in a bowl with the extra virgin olive oil and the thyme leaves. Season with salt and let them rest for 1 hour.

Preheat the oven to 200°C (400°F/gas 6). Tuck the slices of garlic inside the gills of each fish. Roll out half the dough, enough for one thick base, place a fish on one side and fold the dough over to the other to make a half-moon shape and encase the fish, pressing the dough around tightly to seal the edges. Repeat with the second fish. Bake in the preheated oven for 20 minutes.

To remove the fish, insert a knife into the curved edge of the dough and slice around so you can fold back the top layer like a lid. Then fillet the fish using a fork and spoon, not a knife. With the spoon, make an incision lengthways along the centre of each fish, peel back the skin on either side of the incision, and use the fork and spoon to gently pull the flesh way from the bones in two directions. Trying not to break the fillets, lift them off and put them on another plate. When the bones are fully exposed, take hold of the tail and pull the bones up and away from the lower fillet.

Divide the fish over four plates, picking off any remaining bones with tweezers. Pour the tomato and thyme dressing over each plate and serve.

TIME 1 HOUR ● SERVES 4

This is a dish of delicate beauty because the fish sits on a 'crown' of yellow and green zucchini flowers. But there's beauty of flavour too because the fish has a bed of zucchini and garlic. Remember, as ever, to try to find the male zucchini flower, which is the one attached directly to the vine rather than to the end of a zucchini.

16. Pagello con fiori
Goldband snapper with zucchini flowers

3 tbsp olive oil
4 x 180 g (6 oz) fillets goldband
   snapper
4 small zucchini, chopped
1 clove garlic, finely chopped
8 male zucchini flowers
12 mint leaves, finely sliced
   lengthways

Preheat the oven to 160°C (315°F/gas 2–3). Put 1 tablespoon of the olive oil in an ovenproof frying pan, place it over high heat and sear the fish fillets for 1 minute on each side. Then place the frying pan in the preheated oven for 8 minutes.

Meanwhile, heat the remaining 2 tablespoons of olive oil in another frying pan, add the chopped zucchini and sauté for 4 minutes. Reduce the heat, add the chopped garlic and cook for another 3 minutes.

Cut the stems off the zucchini flowers so you have a 'crown'. Cut down one side and open out the flower. Push the zucchini and garlic to one side of the pan. Put the zucchini flowers and the mint leaves into the pan and heat them gently for 30 seconds on each side.

Take the flowers out and spread two on each plate. Place the sautéed zucchini mixture in the middle of each plate and a piece of fish on top, arranged so that the flowers appear to project out from each side of the fish. Serve immediately.

TIME 15 MINUTES • SERVES 4

Ocean trout is a favourite of mine because it is boldly coloured, strongly flavoured and almost as good for you as salmon. Here I'm enhancing its flavour and colour and balancing its plumpness with sharp acidic ingredients. The Italian title of this dish ends with the word for spring, but you can make it any time. Serve it with green beans (see page 24).

17. Trota salmonata primavera
Ocean trout with tomato and lemon zest

5 roma tomatoes, peeled and
    seeded
125 ml (4 fl oz) extra virgin olive oil
zest of 1 lemon, finely sliced
olive oil for frying
4 x 180 g (6 oz) pieces ocean trout
    fillet, skin on
chopped parsley for serving
    (optional)
salt

Chop the tomatoes into small cubes and place them in a bowl. Pour over the extra virgin olive oil and add a little salt and the lemon zest. Toss together and leave to marinate for 1 hour.

Preheat the oven to 180°C (350°F/gas 4). Heat a little olive oil in an ovenproof frying pan, place the fish, skin side down, in the pan and cook for 2 minutes, pressing down on the fish with a fish slice so the skin crisps and doesn't curl. Then sear the other side for 1 minute. Put the pan in the preheated oven for 10 minutes.

To serve, place the fish on the plate, skin side down, and pour over the tomato and lemon mixture. Season to taste. You could sprinkle on a little parsley if you like.

TIME 1 HOUR 10 MINUTES, INCLUDING MARINATING • SERVES 4

You could always skip the quail in this dish and just enjoy the salad. The phrase *al mosto* suggests the salad is dressed with 'must', which is the grape leftovers after wine has been fermented. In fact, we're using a high-class form of 'must' in the form of raspberry vincotto, a luscious vinegar.

18. Quaglie al mosto
Grilled quails with apple and walnut salad

8 quails, deboned and butterflied

FOR THE MARINADE
500 ml (16 fl oz) white wine
   (verdelho or semillon)
4 bay leaves
2 cloves garlic, finely chopped
4 tbsp extra virgin olive oil

FOR THE SALAD
1 large radicchio
1 witlof
1 handful rocket
125 g (4¼ oz) walnuts
2 green apples, cored and finely
   sliced
3 tbsp extra virgin olive oil
1 tbsp raspberry vincotto

Ask the butcher to debone and butterfly the quail. Put them in a large bowl. For the marinade, mix together the white wine, bay leaves, garlic and extra virgin olive oil and pour over the quails. Let them marinate for at least 6 hours.

Preheat the oven to 180°C (350°F/gas 4). Lift the quails out of the marinade, dry them and roast, uncovered, in the preheated oven for 20 minutes (or barbecue them, turning once, and allowing 10 minutes for each side).

To make the salad, pull the radicchio and the witlof apart and place in a bowl with the rocket. Break the walnuts up into pieces and add to the bowl with the sliced apples. Mix together the extra virgin olive oil and the vincotto and pour over the salad. Toss well.

Divide the salad among four plates, place the quails on top and sprinkle over a few more drops of vincotto.

TIME 6 HOURS 30 MINUTES, INCLUDING MARINATING • SERVES 4

If you're a serious vegetarian, you'll want to skip this recipe—or simply ignore the veal and focus on the beetroot with the rocket sauce, which is somewhere between a pesto and a salsa verde. The beetroot and green sauce are ideal accompaniments for hamburgers.

19. Vitello con salsa di rucola e barbabietole
Roast veal with rocket sauce and beetroot

2 beetroot, cleaned and trimmed
300 ml (10 fl oz) extra virgin olive
    oil for marinating
1 tbsp olive oil
1 veal tenderloin, about 700 g (1 lb
    7 oz), cleaned of sinews
salt and freshly ground black
    pepper

FOR THE SAUCE
1 large potato
100 g (3½ oz) rocket
125 ml (4 fl oz) extra virgin olive oil
2 tbsp freshly grated parmesan
    cheese
1 clove garlic, chopped

Boil the beetroot in plenty of water for 15 minutes, strain and peel off the skins. Cut each into about 16 slices, about 1 cm (½ inch) thick. Place in a bowl, and pour over 300 ml (10 fl oz) of extra virgin olive oil. Stir in a little salt and pepper and let them marinate for 3 hours.

Preheat the oven to 200°C (400°F/gas 6). To make the sauce, boil the potato for 20 minutes, then cool a little and peel off the skin. Put the potato in a blender with the rocket leaves, extra virgin olive oil, parmesan and garlic and puree. Set aside.

Put the 1 tablespoon of olive oil in a heavy-based ovenproof frying pan and set over high heat, on top of the stove. Seal the outside of the veal tenderloin, about 2 minutes per side. Then place the pan in the preheated oven and bake, uncovered, for 12 minutes.

Let the veal rest for 4 minutes, then slice it into 12 thick pieces. Place four slices of beetroot in the centre of each plate. Place three slices of veal on top, and pour a line of the green sauce along each.

Whisk a bit of air into the beetroot marinade, which will have turned pink, and drizzle a little around the veal on each plate.

TIME 3 HOURS 30 MINUTES, INCLUDING MARINATING • SERVES 4

This delicious dish is made all over Italy, usually with cream or butter as part of the stuffing. This is the lightest possible version. If you want to make it even lighter, you could use ground almonds instead of the amaretti biscuits.

20. Pesche ripiene
Poached peaches

5 large peaches (slipstone if
   possible)
12 amaretti biscuits
1 egg white
8 tbsp sugar
30 ml (1 fl oz) peach liqueur
8 mint leaves

Preheat the oven to 180°C (350°F/gas 4). Cut four of the peaches in half, remove the stones and slightly hollow out each centre. Crush the amaretti biscuits in a blender, and then add the egg white and blend again to make a coarse paste. With a teaspoon, fill each peach centre with a ball of the amaretti mixture about the size of the original stone.

Line a baking dish with greaseproof paper and place the peach halves on top. Sprinkle with 2 tablespoons of the sugar and bake, uncovered, in the preheated oven for 15 minutes.

Skin the remaining peach and cut it in half. Put the peach halves in a saucepan with 300 ml (10 fl oz) of water and the remaining sugar. Bring to the boil, lower the heat and simmer, uncovered, for 15 minutes. Cool for 10 minutes, then puree with the peach liqueur until smooth.

To serve, pour the puree around the baked peaches and garnish with mint leaves. Serve at room temperature. If you want to be decadent, add a scoop of vanilla ice-cream.

TIME 40 MINUTES • SERVES 4

Italians drive each other crazy by giving away boxes of pannetone (a tall, yellow brioche-type cake) at Christmas time, which means they have to find ways of using up leftover cake in January. In the Southern Hemisphere there are lots of berries around at that time of year, so we have the advantage over Italians in Italy. Here is one suggestion that involves treating slices of pannetone like the base of a pizza. Serve this with a scoop of vanilla ice-cream.

21. Pizza di Natale

Mixed berry 'pizza'

3 kiwifruit, peeled and finely sliced
200 g (6½ oz) strawberries, sliced
200 g (6½ oz) blueberries
400 g (13 oz) raspberries
2 tbsp Maraschino liqueur (or
    other fruit liqueur)
2 tbsp sugar
1 pannetone (or sponge), about
    10 cm (4 inches) in diameter
12 mint leaves, finely chopped

Put the kiwifruit, strawberries, blueberries and half the raspberries in a bowl. Mix together the Maraschino and 1 tablespoon of the sugar and splash it over the fruit. Toss and set aside to macerate for 1 hour.

Slice off four discs of pannetone, each about 2 cm (¾ inch) thick. Place a disc in the middle of four plates. Spoon a mound of the macerated fruit over each slice of pannetone.

Make a coulis by pureeing the remaining raspberries with the remaining sugar and 2 tablespoons of warm water. Drizzle the coulis over and around the mound of fruit on each plate. Sprinkle with the chopped mint.

TIME 1 HOUR 10 MINUTES, INCLUDING MACERATING • SERVES 4

6

the
restaurant
rules

A restaurant is a family. And the happiest of families are those who cook and eat together.

Every afternoon around 5 pm all of us who work in Buon Ricordo set a big table and sit down for a meal—there can be as many as 21 of us. Most nights we do the same thing around midnight, when we are often joined by friends and former staff who are often working at other restaurants around Sydney.

The 5 pm meal gives me the opportunity to review the successes and failures of the previous night, to explain new special dishes and discuss any issues for the night ahead. The late-night meal is an occasion to try out new products and experiments. Sometimes I like to show old Neapolitan dishes to the young chefs—dishes I don't serve to customers, like *Soffritto napoletana*, which is made with trachea, lungs, heart and liver.

There's a long tradition in the restaurant industry of antagonism between the kitchen and front of house, and I find eating together breaks this down and builds up unity, usually amid lots of laughter.

At the table we share our experiences and we learn from them, trying to understand why customers behave the way they do—and, for that matter, why cooks and waiters and owners behave the way they do.

The various chefs take turns to cook for the whole group on different days. I expect an interesting and substantial meal, because if we do not eat well we cannot serve food well.

The shared meal gives the young chefs an opportunity to gain confidence in cooking their own dishes, because we all taste them and give honest reactions. I can keep an eye on the amount of salt the chefs are using and details such as the salad dressing. But mainly I like to be surprised. I am pleased when they draw on their own backgrounds to try something far removed from my Italian origins. That makes 5 o'clock a time of adventure.

Here my cooks share with you some of the meals that have delighted our 21 or so discerning palates and greedy stomachs. You might like to use them when you are entertaining a big group in an informal setting. All the recipes in this chapter are for eight people.

1. **David's sweet and sour rabbit**

2. **Darren's redfish fillets with fregolone**

3. **Darren's double-baked Gruyère cheese soufflé**

4. **Mr Pong's Thai fish salad**

5. **Rosalba's Sicilian fish**

6. **Rosalba's lamb curry**

7. **Michael's chicken congee**

8. **Michael's pasta frittata**

9. **Sean's chicken maryland**

10. **Alexandra's baked kibbeh**

11. **Toru's chicken katsu with seaweed sauce**

12. **Gemma's Middle Eastern chicken**

13. **Armando's spaghetti aglio e olio**

David Wright started with Buon Ricordo as an apprentice, then went off to Italy to gain experience in Don Alfonso restaurant near Sorrento. Now he's come home, a fully qualified chef keen to experiment with dishes such as rabbit done in the classic *agrodolce* (sweet and sour) style. Ask your butcher to cut each rabbit into seven—two legs, two shoulders and the body cut in three—and to give you the livers. You could serve this with mashed potatoes or polenta.

1. David's sweet and sour rabbit

150 ml (5 fl oz) olive oil
2 rabbits, each cut into 7 pieces
   (see above), with livers
4 onions, sliced
5 large desiree potatoes, peeled and
   cut into chunks
5 tbsp brown sugar
250 ml (8 fl oz) white wine vinegar
1 handful roughly chopped parsley
salt and freshly ground black
   pepper

Preheat the oven to 180°C (350°F/gas 4). Put about 50 ml (1¾ fl oz) of the olive oil into a large ovenproof frying pan, place it over high heat and brown the pieces of rabbit for about 5 minutes, turning them often. Take out the rabbit pieces and set aside, with the livers (which need the least amount of cooking) separate.

Add the remaining olive oil to the pan, and sauté the onions and potatoes over medium heat for 10 minutes, stirring often. Then put back the rabbit pieces (but not the livers). Stir the sugar into the vinegar, then pour it over the rabbit. Scrape up any rabbit bits stuck to the bottom of the pan and stir it into the sauce.

Cover the pan with foil and place in the preheated oven. Every 10 minutes or so, pour in about 60 ml (2 fl oz) of water. After 30 minutes, add the reserved livers. After a further 15 minutes, remove the pan from the oven, season with salt and pepper and arrange the pieces of rabbit and the livers on a large platter. Pour everything left in the pan over the rabbit and sprinkle over the chopped parsley. Let your guests serve themselves from the platter.

TIME 1 HOUR • SERVES 8

Darren Taylor is the senior chef in my kitchen, with French training now adapted to Italian philosophy. He has also been a good friend for many years. It gives me enormous pleasure to be able to work with him and exchange ideas. Here are two of his recipes, one using *fregolone* pasta, a kind of couscous popular in Sardinia, and the second a classically French soufflé. Serve this with green salad and sourdough bread for dipping.

2. Darren's redfish fillets with fregolone

2 cloves garlic, peeled
60 ml (2 fl oz) extra virgin olive oil
100 g (3½ oz) black olives, pitted
  and halved
1 kg (2 lb) tinned tomatoes,
  crushed
25 g (1 oz) capers, washed
1 tbsp chilli oil
250 g (8 oz) *fregolone*
vegetable oil for frying
1 kg (2 lb) redfish fillets, skinned
  and boned
flour for dusting
1 tbsp chopped parsley
salt

Put the whole garlic cloves in a frying pan with the extra virgin olive oil and sauté over medium heat until golden, about 2 minutes. Discard the garlic. Add the olives and sauté for another 3 minutes. Add the tomatoes, bring to the boil, lower the heat and simmer gently for 45 minutes. Stir in the capers and a little chilli oil, to your taste.

Add some salt to a large saucepan of boiling water, toss in the *fregolone* and cook until *al dente*, about 15 minutes.

At the same time, heat 6 cm (2½ inches) of vegetable oil in a wok or deep frying pan until it sizzles when a drop of water is thrown in. Toss the fish fillets in flour and deep-fry them in the oil until they are golden, about 4 minutes. Place the fillets on paper towels. Sprinkle on a little salt.

Drain the *fregolone* and stir them into the tomato sauce. Divide this among eight plates, and arrange the fish fillets on top. Sprinkle the fish with the chopped parsley.

TIME 1 HOUR 10 MINUTES • SERVES 8

This soufflé is cooked in the oven once, then chilled, then topped with even more Gruyère and put back into a very hot oven. Darren says the smellier the cheese, the better it all tastes. He concedes that it might even taste better if you used half Gruyère and half grated parmesan.

3. Darren's double-baked Gruyère cheese soufflé

125 g (4¼ oz) flour, sieved
pinch of nutmeg
1 tsp mustard powder
125 g (4¼ oz) unsalted butter
600 ml (20 fl oz) milk
700 g (1 lb 7 oz) Gruyère cheese,
    grated
8 egg yolks
12 egg whites
clarified butter for buttering
    moulds
600 ml (19 fl oz) cream
20 stems of chives, finely chopped
pinch of salt
freshly ground black pepper

8 x soufflé moulds, 6 cm diameter x
    9 cm deep (2½ x 3½ inches)

Preheat the oven to 180°C (350°C/gas 4). In a bowl, mix together the flour, nutmeg and mustard powder. Make a roux by melting the unsalted butter in a saucepan and adding the seasoned flour. Cook slowly over low heat, stirring often with a wooden spoon until you have a sandy consistency. Add the milk slowly, whisking as you do so. Cook on low heat for 4 minutes, stirring the whole time. Add 400 g (13 oz) of the grated Gruyère and then the egg yolks. Remove from the heat and continue stirring for 2 minutes. Pour the mixture into a large bowl.

In a separate bowl, beat the egg whites with a pinch of salt until you have soft peaks. With a rubber spatula, fold the egg whites into the cheese mixture, a little at a time.

Butter the soufflé moulds with the clarified butter and spoon in the mixture. Place the moulds in a deep-sided baking dish and pour water into the dish so it reaches about halfway up the sides of the moulds. Bake the soufflés in the preheated oven until they are golden on top, about 30 minutes. Take them out of the oven and place the moulds on a rack.

When cool, turn the soufflés out onto a buttered baking dish. If the soufflé sticks to the sides of the moulds, run a small knife around the sides to release it. You can put the soufflés into the fridge until you are ready to serve them.

When you are ready to finish the dish, preheat the oven to 200°C (400°F/gas 6). Pour the cream over the soufflés and sprinkle over the remaining Gruyère. Bake in the oven for 20 minutes.

To serve, place each soufflé in the centre of a warm serving plate, spoon some creamy sauce over it and sprinkle with the chopped chives and freshly ground black pepper.

TIME 1 HOUR • SERVES 8

We call him Mr Pong because it takes too long to say Veerapong Thirapathompong. He has been a loyal member of my team since 1990, when he arrived from Thailand. His expertise is deep-frying and he is the master of dishes such as crispy prawns, calzone and zucchini flowers in batter. In this case, he fries fish pieces with a spectacular salad.

4. Mr Pong's Thai fish salad

250 g (8 oz) carrots, finely sliced
250 g (8 oz) celery, finely sliced
300 g (10 oz) bean sprouts
250 g (8 oz) snowpeas or sugar
    snap peas
1 small head iceberg lettuce,
    roughly sliced
50 g (1¾ oz) fresh ginger, very
    finely sliced
2 handfuls coriander leaves,
    chopped
1 handful mint leaves, chopped
1 tbsp chopped basil leaves
1 kg (2 lb) white fish, such as
    flathead or silver dory
flour for dusting
vegetable oil for frying
125 g (4¼ oz) roasted shelled
    peanuts, crushed

FOR THE SAUCE
250 ml (8 fl oz) sweet chilli sauce
50 ml (1¾ oz) fish sauce
25 ml (1 fl oz) soy sauce
juice of 2 lemons

Mix together the vegetables, ginger and herbs in a large bowl and arrange on a large serving platter.

Clean and cut the fish into pieces about 3 cm (1¼ inch) square, then coat them lightly with flour. Heat 6 cm (2½ inches) of vegetable oil in a wok or deep frying pan until it sizzles when a drop of water is thrown in and deep-fry the fish until crispy, about 10 minutes. Drain on paper towels, then place the fish pieces on top of the vegetables.

For the sauce, bring the chilli, fish and soy sauces to the boil in a large saucepan and pour over the fish and vegetables. Add lemon juice to taste and top with the crushed peanuts.

TIME 20 MINUTES • SERVES 8

Rosalba Bertocci is a beautiful, fiery chef of Sicilian background. She started with me as an apprentice and I now have great satisfaction in watching her run the meat section. Here she offers a Sicilian classic and on page 222 something spicier from further afield. Boiled potatoes are the perfect accompaniment to this dish.

5. Rosalba's Sicilian fish

1 kg (2 lb) firm fish, such as
    flathead or warehou
2 medium Spanish onions, sliced
2 large celery sticks, sliced
4 whole cloves garlic
2 or 3 red chillies, chopped
200 ml (6½ fl oz) olive oil
150 g (5 oz) capers
150 g (5 oz) black olives, pitted
500 ml (16 fl oz) white wine
5 large tomatoes, chopped
200 ml (6½ fl oz) tomato puree
2 handfuls parsley, coarsely
    chopped
1 tbsp coarsely chopped basil leaves
salt and freshly ground black
    pepper

Cut the fish into large pieces about 6 cm (2½ inches) in length. Preheat the oven to 150°C (300°F/gas 2).

In a large ovenproof frying pan, sauté the onions, celery, garlic and chilli in the olive oil on top of the stove over medium heat until soft, about 10 minutes. Add the capers and black olives and continue cooking for another 5 minutes. Add the pieces of fish and turn to cook on all sides, in total about 5 minutes. Add the wine and simmer for another 5 minutes to evaporate the alcohol. Add the chopped tomatoes and tomato puree and cook until soft but not mushy, about 3 minutes. Season with salt and freshly ground black pepper.

Cover the pan with foil and bake in the preheated oven for 15 minutes. Sprinkle over the chopped parsley and basil.

TIME 45 MINUTES ● SERVES 8

This is an Indian dish, a mild but full-flavoured curry. You can use more chilli, but then you'd risk missing the subtleties of the spices. Serve it with plain basmati rice and yoghurt.

6. Rosalba's lamb curry

3 medium onions, roughly chopped
5 tbsp olive oil
1 tbsp finely chopped fresh ginger
1 bird's eye chilli, seeded and sliced
8 garlic cloves, crushed
1 heaped tbsp ground cinnamon
1 heaped tbsp ground cumin
1 heaped tbsp ground turmeric
1 heaped tbsp ground coriander
1 kg (2 lb) lamb shoulder or leg, in
    2-cm (¾-inch) cubes
500 g (1 lb) roma tomatoes,
    roughly chopped (or use tinned)
1 bay leaf
120 g (4 oz) almond meal
salt and freshly ground black
    pepper

Put the onions and oil in a large casserole dish and sauté over medium heat for 5 minutes, then add the ginger, chilli and garlic and cook until browned, another 5 minutes. Add all the remaining spices and sauté for another 2 minutes, stirring constantly with a wooden spoon, until the aromas start to be released. Add the lamb pieces, a few at a time, and brown on all sides. Then add the chopped tomatoes, bay leaf and enough water to cover the meat. Simmer, covered, for 3 hours over low heat.

Just before serving, stir in the almond meal to thicken the sauce.

TIME 3 HOURS 15 MINUTES • SERVES 8

Michael Van Heynsbergen is the backbone of our kitchen. He started working with me at my first Sydney restaurant, Pulcinella, 25 years ago. He learned Italian flavours from my parents and met his wife in our kitchen. Michael specialises in superb sauces, but here he ventures to China, and then returns to Italy for a convenient way of using up leftover pasta (on page 224).

7. Michael's chicken congee

1 x 1.5 kg (3 lb) chicken
125 g (4¼ oz) fresh ginger
1 handful coriander stalks, finely
    chopped
1 medium carrot, thinly sliced
1 stick celery, thinly sliced
½ red capsicum, thinly sliced
3 bird's eye chillies, seeded and
    chopped
2 tbsp coarsely chopped coriander
    leaves
25 ml (1 fl oz) soy sauce
25 ml (1 fl oz) fish sauce
500 g (1 lb) long-grain rice
flour for dusting
75 ml (2½ fl oz) peanut oil
salt and freshly ground black
    pepper

Place the chicken in a large saucepan and cover it with water. Add 75 g (2½ oz) of the grated ginger and the finely chopped coriander stalks. Bring to the boil and simmer until the chicken falls off the bones, about 1 hour. Remove the chicken from the saucepan and strip the meat off the bones. Shred the meat and separate it into two equal parts. Return the bones to the pan and continue simmering the stock for 2 hours.

For the garnish, grate the remaining ginger and place it in a bowl with the carrot, celery, capsicum, chillies and chopped coriander leaves. Mix with the soy and fish sauces.

Strain the stock and discard the bones. Add the rice to the stock and simmer it gently, uncovered, until it has a porridge-like consistency, about 50 minutes. In the last 5 minutes, stir in half the chicken meat. Add a little more water if the rice seems to be drying out.

Toss the other half of the chicken meat in a little flour. Heat the peanut oil in a large frying pan until it is very hot. Add the floured chicken meat, and fry until crisp and golden. Just before serving, spoon the garnish over the rice porridge and sprinkle the crispy chicken over that. Season to taste.

TIME 4 HOURS • SERVES 8

This type of pie is a great way to use up any pasta and vegetables you have left. Don't worry too much about precise quantities. The point is to play with the ingredients you already have.

8. Michael's pasta frittata

250 g (8 oz) shelled fresh peas (or frozen)
500 g (1 lb) long pasta (spaghetti or fettuccine), broken into small pieces
8 eggs
250 g (8 oz) grated parmesan cheese
3 roma tomatoes, chopped
150 g (5 oz) pancetta (or bacon), cut into small cubes
4 basil leaves, sliced
olive oil for cooking
salt and freshly ground black pepper

Preheat the oven to 200°C (400°F/gas 6). If the peas are fresh, cook them in a saucepan of boiling water for 6 minutes; if they are frozen, boil for 3 minutes. If the pasta is not already cooked, break it into roughly 3-cm (1¼-inch) lengths and cook in a large saucepan of boiling salted water for about 7 minutes. Beat the eggs well, add the drained pasta, peas, parmesan, tomatoes, pancetta and basil. Mix well and season with salt and pepper to taste.

Pour a little olive oil in a large ovenproof frying pan and place on high heat. Pour in the egg mixture and leave to cook for 2 minutes without stirring, then place the pan in the preheated oven for 10 minutes.

Remove the pan from the oven. Hold a plate on top of the frying pan and turn the frittata upside down onto the plate. Put the frying pan on top of the stove over medium heat, add a little more olive oil, and slide the frittata back into the pan so what was the top is now bottom down. Place it back in the oven until the frittata is browned on top, about 7 minutes. Turn it out onto a plate and cut into wedges. Serve hot or cold with salad.

TIME 40 MINUTES • SERVES 8

Sean Mawbey was an apprentice from the countryside when he started with us—strong, enthusiastic and eager to absorb what an Italian kitchen can offer. He is now well qualified and has travelled to Europe to further his education, leaving behind this recipe. This is good with a lettuce salad.

9. Sean's chicken maryland

5 onions, sliced thinly
75 ml (2½ fl oz) olive oil
750 g (1 lb 8 oz) desiree potatoes, peeled and diced
2 tbsp chopped rosemary
8 chicken marylands (thigh and drumstick)
salt and freshly ground black pepper

Preheat the oven to 200°C (400°F/gas 6). In a frying pan, sauté the onions in the olive oil for 5 minutes over high heat, then lower the heat and cook gently for another 20 minutes until the onions become tender and sweet. Transfer to a baking dish and add the potatoes and rosemary.

Put the chicken pieces, skin side down, in the frying pan over high heat and crisp the skin, about 5 minutes. Turn the pieces over and seal the other side for 2 minutes. Place the chicken pieces, skin side up, on top of the potatoes in the baking dish, and roast in the preheated oven for 25 minutes.

Divide the chicken pieces among eight plates, season the potatoes with salt and pepper, and compose the mixture around each piece of chicken.

TIME 1 HOUR • SERVES 8

Alexandra Rispoli has Italian in her heritage. She started with Buon Ricordo as an apprentice and now specialises in desserts. In fact, she is on her way to becoming Sydney's finest pastry chef. This is a kind of Lebanese meat loaf. Its main ingredient is lamb, which is prepared in two ways so that the dish has layers. The kibbeh is served with a tahini-based sauce and a refreshing salad of parsley, tomatoes and cucumber.

10. Alexandra's baked kibbeh

500 g (1 lb) rough burghul wheat
750 g (1 lb 8 oz) minced lamb
2 tsp salt
2 medium onions, chopped
1 tsp ground black pepper
1 tsp ground allspice
1 tsp ground cinnamon
1 clove garlic, finely chopped
50 g (1¾ oz) butter, plus extra for
    topping

FOR THE FILLING
60 ml (2 fl oz) olive oil
250 g (8 oz) lamb, finely chopped
1 onion, finely chopped
1 clove garlic, finely chopped
1 tsp ground allspice
1 tsp ground cinnamon
1 tsp ground nutmeg
125 g (4¼ oz) pine nuts and/or
    pistachio nuts, shelled
salt and white pepper

FOR THE SAUCE
250 g (8 oz) plain yoghurt
100 g (3½ oz) tahini
juice of 1 lemon
50 ml (1¾ fl oz) olive oil
1 small clove garlic, mashed to a
    paste
salt and freshly ground black
    pepper

Preheat the oven to 180°C (350°F/gas 4). Put the burghul wheat in a bowl, cover with water and soak for 15 minutes.

While the burghul is soaking, make the filling. Heat the olive oil in a frying pan and brown the chopped lamb over high heat for about 5 minutes. Add the onion and cook for another 5 minutes, then add the garlic and cook for another 3 minutes. Add the spices and finally the nuts. Season with salt and pepper to taste.

Drain the burghul and mix it with the minced lamb, salt, chopped onions, ground black pepper, allspice, cinnamon, garlic and the 50 g (1¾ oz) of butter. Knead the mixture with your hands to make a dough, gradually adding water until it becomes smooth.

Oil a large baking dish and, with wet hands, press half the burghul mixture evenly over the base of the dish. Then spread the cooked filling evenly over the burghul. Top with the other half of the burghul mix, spreading evenly. Make incisions across the mixture so it is divided into diamond shapes. Dot with bits of butter.

Bake the kibbeh, uncovered, in the preheated oven for 1 hour. Just before serving, mix together all the sauce ingredients. Serve the kibbeh cut into diamonds on a big platter with the bowl of sauce and a green salad with cucumbers and tomatoes.

TIME 1 HOUR 30 MINUTES • SERVES 8

Toru Ryu was recommended to me by my friend Tetsuya Wakuda, of Tetsuya's restaurant in Sydney. Toru was eager to learn about Italian cooking and compare it with Japanese techniques. Like most Japanese chefs, he has a sensitive palate and is very precise in his work. He specialises in seafood.

11. Toru's chicken katsu with seaweed sauce

40 g (1½ oz) kombu seaweed
100 g (3½ oz) dry bonito
125 ml (4 fl oz) mirin
100 ml (3½ fl oz) sake
125 ml (4 fl oz) soy sauce
20 g (¾ oz) sugar
2 medium onions, thinly sliced
30 g (1 oz) cornflour
1.2 kg (2 lb 6 oz) chicken thighs
100 g (3½ oz) flour
6 eggs
250 g (8 oz) dry breadcrumbs
olive oil for frying
½ bunch shallots, thinly sliced, for garnish
salt and freshly ground black pepper

To prepare the sauce, place the kombu seaweed in a large saucepan with about 2 litres (72 fl oz) of water and slowly bring to the boil. Turn the heat down so it simmers gently for 30 minutes.

Using tongs, take out the seaweed and add the bonito to the water. Turn off the heat and let it sit for 10 minutes. Skim off any impurities floating to the top, then strain the liquid into a new saucepan. This is known as dashi stock. Add the mirin, sake, soy sauce and sugar to the stock. Bring to the boil and simmer for 10 minutes. Add the sliced onions and cook for a further 5 minutes.

Using a fork, mix the cornflour with 60 ml (2 fl oz) of water until smooth. While the sauce is boiling, add the cornflour mixture in a slow stream. Mix and stir constantly until it becomes thick. Bring back to the boil to cook the cornflour, about 2 minutes.

Meanwhile, open up the chicken thighs and flatten the meat so that it cooks more quickly. Put the flour into a bowl and season with a little salt and pepper. Lightly beat two of the eggs in a second bowl. Put the breadcrumbs in a third bowl. Dip each piece of chicken into the flour, then the egg, then the breadcrumbs. Heat a little olive oil in a frying pan and fry the chicken until golden, about 6 minutes.

When you are about to serve the dish, lightly beat the remaining eggs and add them to the boiling sauce. Cook gently for a further 1 minute. Serve the chicken on steamed rice with the sauce poured over and sprinkled with the sliced shallots.

TIME: 1 HOUR • SERVES 8

Gemma Cunningham is Buon Ricordo's manager and the first face customers see when they walk in the door. She is also my wife. Here she draws on her mother's Lebanese background to spice up a chicken stew. The most exotic ingredient is the pomegranate molasses.

12. Gemma's Middle Eastern chicken

2 white onions, chopped
2 carrots, diced
6 tbsp olive oil
2 x 1.5 kg (3 lb) fat hens (preferably organic), each cut into 8 pieces
2 tsp cayenne pepper
2 tsp ground allspice
6 tbsp pomegranate molasses
125 ml (4 fl oz) brandy
2 pomegranates
salt and freshly ground black pepper

Preheat the oven to 180°C (350°F/gas 4). Cook the onions and carrots with the olive oil in a large casserole dish over low heat until the onions are soft, about 10 minutes. Turn up the heat, add the chicken pieces and brown, turning often, about 5 minutes. When all the chicken is browned, return the pieces to the casserole. Add the cayenne pepper and allspice and stir for 1 minute. Add 3 tablespoons of the pomegranate molasses and 60 ml (2 fl oz) of the brandy. Cover the pan with foil and place it in the preheated oven for 45 minutes. Check every 10 minutes, turning the chicken pieces and adding 125 ml (4 fl oz) of water if it is drying out.

Take the casserole dish out of the oven and place it on top of the stove over low heat. Add the remaining molasses and brandy along with the pomegranate seeds and pulp. Cook over medium heat for 3 minutes to evaporate the alcohol. Season to taste and serve with plain rice.

TIME 1 HOUR 10 MINUTES • SERVES 8

We love to eat this at midnight after a hard day's work. Italian families traditionally join in this 'pasta toss up' to recover after a long lunch or dinner. It keeps the party going a little longer and it's a helpful hangover treatment in anticipation of the next morning.

13. Armando's spaghetti aglio e olio

600 g (1 lb 3½ oz) spaghetti
250 ml (8 fl oz) extra virgin olive oil
2 small hot chillies, seeded and finely chopped
3 cloves garlic, chopped finely
1 handful parsley, coarsely chopped
salt

Bring a large saucepan of water to the boil, add 1 tablespoon of salt and return to the boil. Add the pasta and cook until *al dente*, about 6 minutes. Drain.

When the pasta is cooked, heat the olive oil in a frying pan, add the chillies and sauté for 1 minute. Add the garlic and cook until golden, about 2 minutes. Immediately add the pasta and toss for a minute so the strands are thoroughly coated with the flavoured olive oil. Add the parsley, toss and season with salt. Serve. The pasta is meant to be quite oily.

TIME 15 MINUTES • SERVES 8

Index

Acknowledgements

I want to dedicate this book to my family, over five generations.

My grandparents—Carmella and Armando, Antonio and Raffaela—showed me the importance of respecting tradition in cooking and quality in ingredients, while my mother Olimpia and my father Mario showed me how to care for customers.

My wife Gemma has made it possible for Buon Ricordo to thrive. I must confess to being a moody character, but she is consistent in her warmth, kindness and patience.

My dear children Antonella, Mario and Sascha have given me so much joy, and I am delighted that all of them, in one way or another, have ended up in the hospitality business. I look to my grandchildren—Christian, Freya and Dante—as the future of a family that lives to cook.

In making this book, my special thanks go to David Dale, who understood exactly what I needed to say and was able to find the essence of my ideas inside my individual approach to the English language. I would also like to acknowledge the help of my staff in developing many of these recipes, and the inspiration of my friend Tetsuya Wakuda.

For having the faith to commission the book, I thank Sue Hines and, for massive efforts in producing it, I thank editors Mary Trewby and Alexandra Nahlous, and designer Marylouise Brammer. For the beautiful images, I thank photographer Greg Elms and the stylist Virginia Dowzer.

And I am grateful to all our faithful customers—even the ones I've had occasion to argue with over the years. They have responded with eagerness to my new approaches to Italian tradition. I doubt if my attempts at innovation would have been encouraged so enthusiastically in the land of my birth.

I love Australia because it is an open-minded society with a spirit of adventure. As my co-author likes to say, I am living in Italy's most successful colony.

Armando Percuoco